Crystal Magic

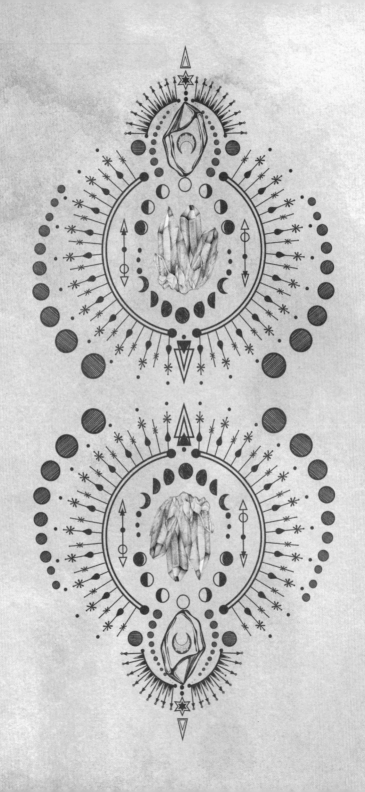

Crystal Magic

A Practical Handbook on
THE POWER OF
SACRED STONES

AURORA KANE

WELLFLEET
PRESS

For John

Inspiring | Educating | Creating | Entertaining

Brimming with creative inspiration, how-to projects, and useful information to enrich your everyday life, quarto.com is a favorite destination for those pursuing their interests and passions.

© 2022 Quarto Publishing Group USA Inc.

First published in 2022 by Wellfleet Press, an imprint of The Quarto Group, 142 West 36th Street, 4th Floor, New York, NY 10018, USA T (212) 779-4972 F (212) 779-6058 www.Quarto.com

Wellfleet titles are also available at discount for retail, wholesale, promotional, and bulk purchase. For details, contact the Special Sales Manager by email at specialsales@quarto.com or by mail at The Quarto Group, Attn: Special Sales Manager, 100 Cummings Center Suite 265D, Beverly, MA 01915 USA

10 9 8 7 6 5 4 3 2 1

ISBN: 978-1-57715-293-4

Library of Congress Cataloging-in-Publication Data

Names: Kane, Aurora, author.
Title: Crystal magic : a practical handbook on the power of sacred stones / Aurora Kane.
Description: New York, NY, USA : Wellfleet Press, [2022] | Series: Mystical handbook | Includes bibliographical references and index. | Summary: "A spellbook and comprehensive guide to the inherent magic in these sacred stones, Crystal Magic guides witches through the practical use of one of their favorite materials"-- Provided by publisher.
Identifiers: LCCN 2022002758 (print) | LCCN 2022002759 (ebook) | ISBN 9781577152934 (hardcover) | ISBN 9780760374429 (ebook)
Subjects: LCSH: Crystals--Miscellanea. | Magic.
Classification: LCC BF1442.C78 K36 2022 (print) | LCC BF1442.C78 (ebook)
 | DDC 133/.2548--dc23/eng/20220225
LC record available at https://lccn.loc.gov/2022002758
LC ebook record available at https://lccn.loc.gov/2022002759

Publisher: Rage Kindelsperger
Creative Director: Laura Drew
Managing Editor: Cara Donaldson
Editor: Elizabeth You
Layout Design: Sydney Martenis

Printed in China

Contents

LET YOUR MAGIC SPARKLE!

Imagine you're surrounded by a gem in every hue;
their brilliant glow and beauty are, at first, what call to you.

Look closer and you'll see the lines of wisdom on their face—
the clues to how they've come to be that mark their time and place.

Held gently in your hand, you feel a whisper back in time
that speaks of ancient secrets known, just waiting now to shine.

Their spark within a wink that says they recognize you, too,
for kindred magic spirits see the shining light in you.

What destiny ordained the path that led you to this place—where
crystals dwell and magic swells the dreams we do embrace?

Get ready to be dazzled by the sparkle you create—
with crystal magic energies, success is now your fate!

Give thanks to Mother Earth and all the treasures she bestows.
These crystals are but evidence of all we've yet to know.

As above, so below.

Introduction

C an you feel it? The vibrations are growing stronger, like the joyful beating of your heart or the truth of your intentions about to be unleashed. For crystal magic grows within Earth's heart, absorbing her energies, wisdom, magic, and power destined to find just the right spirit to connect with once revealed.

Welcome to the beautiful, mystical, magical world of crystal magic. Whether in natural form just plucked from Earth, polished and set as jewelry to adorn, rough and tumbled to be used as decoration, carved and intended as a talisman, or any other form to delight, crystals bring a wealth of energy and inspiring beauty to our world that is a treasure to behold. Here, we'll learn to unlock their secrets and healing energies to boost intuition, clear channels of communication, and release all kinds of magical energies into the universe for manifesting intentions, achieving goals, and living a sparkling, spellbinding life.

An appreciation, even adoration, of crystals for their intrinsic beauty, rarity, value, and power has existed for millennia, and has grown and evolved over time. Crystals' uses as ancient symbols, amulets, talismans, adornments, and for building wealth transforms today into alternative healing practices, international industry, beautiful jewelry, and, of course, magical practices.

Crystals' journey from creation to discovery is as magical as their energies, and the fate that puts them in your hands is proof that magic exists. Crystals can help us see into the past, with the ancient messages they carry, as well as into the future, if we're willing to look. They can also help us see the present more clearly and hold our intentions firmly in sight as we work to make them real.

Here we'll learn a bit about how crystals form their place in history and how to harness their innate energy to boost your magical workings and create a healing presence in your life. We'll look at where the magic starts by setting crystal clear intentions. Then, we will go on to explore ways to incorporate crystal magic into your existing rituals, adding new ideas along the way.

We'll learn about forty-six crystals in more detail, including the language they speak and how to use their vibrational energies to raise your own energies and see the many manifest ways they can help you achieve the brilliant, sparkling life you've planned to live. Thirty-three meditations, rituals, and spells round out the journey to help you get started or reignite the spark within.

I see an amazing future for you!

A Sparkling Magical Life

Created through millennia in the heart of Earth, absorbing her energies and messages along with those sent by the Sun, Moon, and oceans, natural crystals and gemstones hold that power and emit those energies, helping raise your personal vibration and enhancing your psychic and intuitive powers. They contain the natural pulse of the Earth, the breath of the Earth, and they can speak to you if you listen. When Earth reveals her treasures to us, they bear stories of connection. They grow from water rich in dissolved minerals, melted rock, and even vapor. Time, temperature, and pressure shift and mold them into dazzlingly beautiful colors and forms, just as these same forces shift and mold us through a lifetime. Crystals are the ultimate survivors and, thus, can be extremely powerful forces in our lives. Adding crystals and their unique energies to your magical practice helps harness their innate powers and amplify your intentions to uniquely empower your life.

CRYSTALS DEFINED

Crystals form deep within Earth through a process called crystallization, where a solid grows from a liquid (through cooling and/or evaporation), or even a gas. The term *crystal* derives from the Greek word *krystallos*, meaning ice, or crystal.

The scientific definition of a *true* crystal is a solid object whose basic structure repeats in a consistent, ordered geometric pattern (called a lattice) that extends both internally and to the surface. Crystals, in magical practice, include true crystals that have this scientifically defined molecular composition, such as salt, some gemstones, snowflakes, and clear quartz—likely the first thing that comes to mind when you think "crystal"—and exhibit a type of sacred geometry (see page 74). Crystals in your magical practice also include organic rocks, stones, minerals, and other fossilized materials, like petrified wood; these may look like but are not scientifically "true" crystals, which in no way diminishes their energy, beauty, power, or value.

This definition of crystals is broad and at its magical center is the inherent energy of the stones: the same energy that is in the wind and oceans, moonlight and sunlight, laughter and music, color and the rainbow, herbs and flowers. Crystals, as with all natural things, vibrate with their unique energy and amplify the energies surrounding them. They are a conduit for transmitting energy to the Universe and can receive the energy you ask them to hold.

CRYSTALS IN HISTORY

It's hard to imagine whoever first discovered crystals as a gift from the Earth wasn't as fascinated and captivated by their beauty and variety as we are today.

Using crystals as a part of daily life and for their powers of healing is credited as far back as six thousand years to the Mesopotamians, and organic beads and amulets, such as those made from amber or carved from animal teeth, have been traced back tens of thousands of years earlier to places far and wide around the world. Records tell us that traditional Chinese medicine has employed crystals for healing as far back as five thousand years. In Indian beliefs, crystals have long been revered for their healing and balancing properties.

Crystals and gemstones have certainly adorned and enriched the wealthy and powerful for centuries, and have even been believed to influence the wearer's aura in some respects, such as to make one more powerful, agreeable, mesmerizing, strong, or knowledgeable.

The ancient Sumerians wrote of using crystals in magical formulas and the ancient Greeks used them in jewelry and as charms and talismans for protection and health, in this world and the next—and even as cosmetics, grinding them into a powder to color or line the eyes and face.

As their uses and lore grew across cultures, crystals were often paired with herbal remedies for healing, and meanings were ascribed to crystals based on name origin, like "amethyst" meaning "not drunk." So, this crystal was frequently worn as an amulet to protect against inebriation.

Probably not unrelated, magical tales of crystals' use in spells and witchcraft have traveled the world for centuries. As a gift from Earth, it makes sense that practitioners of religions based in Nature and her principles would incorporate them into their rituals and recognize them for the power they hold.

Today, crystals enjoy a wide popularity for use in alternative healing practices, to energize physical spaces and to manifest intentions with their powerful energies. Here, we will specifically look at using crystals as part of your magical life to enhance the power of your intentions and to live a life of dazzling radiance and joy.

Talisman or Amulet?

The use of talismans and amulets dates back thousands of years, and these two magical words are often used interchangeably. Although their actual uses are similar, depending on your intentions, there are subtle differences to consider. Regardless of which you may need, crystals make a wonderful, and historical, option when chosen carefully—and with intent or intuition.

Talismans, typically, are carved or otherwise enhanced to add to their energies and are used in the belief that they bring greater power to their owner.

Amulets, on the other hand, are frequently worn or carried as a sort of protective device, to keep away harm or to protect from evil influences—such as that all-feared evil eye.

And, not to be forgotten, there are charms . . . said to draw luck to you.

CRYSTAL ENERGIES

The natural vibrations emanating from crystals are believed by some to promote healing, acting as a gateway to both disperse negative energy and allow positive energy to flow in to replace it. It is the same power seen in all natural forces, with the same origins, understood intuitively and nurtured with truth and belief. It is a palpable energy that is not only powerful on its own, but can also influence the energies around it. It is an energy released by our intentions and one that returns to us in their manifestations. When you invite crystals into your life, do so with an open, receptive mind and heart and the power of your intentions. They will respond in kind.

Crystals that formed slowly over time emit gentler energy vibrations than crystals formed from cosmic force or explosion, whose energies are more intense and immediate. When you connect with the individual energies of crystals to bring their magical influence into your practice, you can create a purposeful life that manifests not only intentions but also true peace and contentment. When you focus your energies and intentions on your crystals, the crystals hold them there, inside, reminding you—by their very presence—what is important to you.

SELECTING CRYSTALS AND GEMSTONES

Crystals come in a multitude of types, shapes, colors, sizes, uses, vibrational energies, and prices, which means choosing which crystals to add to your life is a personal decision. Crystals can be in raw form, tumbled, carved, or polished and faceted, as in jewelry or other objects. Large or small, it doesn't matter. And they don't have to be expensive. Many are commonly available.

In addition to the inherent fire and beauty we find in crystals and gemstones, it's their unique power, energy, and meaning that become truly magical when combined with your energy. Take time to research crystals based on your circumstances and needs, and their source (see page 84 for more).

Start with that special crystal that speaks strongly to you, whether through an instinctive pull or the crystal's beauty, sentimental value, vibrational energy, historical use, or energetic abilities. Maybe you feel the special power of your birthstone or the unexpected connection with a particular stone given to you as a gift or an heirloom. Build a magical treasure chest slowly. Or select crystals to work with based on your desired intentions, which means they'll change as you do. You can't choose wrong. As you build your magical crystal jewel box, it is your chance to experiment and be creative about achieving the results you desire. Trust your gut. That is your intuition at work, recognizing what you need even if you're unsure.

Whether you wear your crystals in the form of jewelry or carry them with you is purely a matter of preference. Or just let them be, placed near you on your desk or altar, in the room where you meditate or sleep, or on a windowsill to guard against negative energy entering your space. However you need them to be, they will be there with you. Get to know each crystal's basic personality, and select the ones you feel "in tune" with. Start basic and grow from there.

Tuning in to Crystal Magic

Each crystal's energy is uniquely powerful and each crystal brings its specific charm and personality to your magical workings. Working with crystals is an active process of getting to know them and then tending to them to keep their energies flowing. But before any magic can be accomplished with them, knowing your true intentions for working with crystals requires the willingness to look honestly into your heart, even if your head tries to overrule you, and committing to working toward your truest manifestation of self. Crystal energies are powerful, and when combined with your powerful energies, the combination is magical.

SETTING CRYSTAL CLEAR INTENTIONS

All action springs from intention—and intentions, like all things, are made of energy, which connects us universally. This energy is the reason we can unite so powerfully with crystal energy to multiply our magic and influence what we manifest. Setting clear intentions is really the first step to activating your magical powers, especially when working with crystals, so that which you seek can be amplified with crystal energies. For when you combine a crystal's ancient wisdom and innate vibrations to manifest specific energies with your intentional energies, true magic crystalizes in your life.

To clearly define your intentions, consider:

- What do you seek?

- What do you need?

- What do you wish to accomplish?

- What needs attention in your life?

- What might you need to let go of?

- Where does it hurt so it may be healed?

- What gives you joy?

Reach deep into your soul to acknowledge, without fear or judgment, what is important to you and what will make you truly happy. Call upon your favorite crystals so you can absorb their energy and lessons and to bring clarity to your thoughts.

Setting specific intentions based on these self-defined priorities creates goals aligned with your values and dreams. Defining intentions keeps you focused and living in the present, mindfully, and can help improve your overall well-being. Important, too, is living mindfully without judgment, learning to accept what is and working to change circumstances, as you desire.

Remember, intentions change as we change. Don't be afraid to adjust, replace, or refine them as your needs and priorities evolve. Stay true to yourself in seeking your dreams and desires.

IS ANYONE LISTENING?

When you release your intentions into the Universe, the vibrational energy ripples cause chain reactions that can take time to reveal themselves. Results may be delayed—or not what you expected—but likely are there if you look and listen carefully. If, however, you really feel a universal cold shoulder, pause for a moment in a quiet place, take a look within, and make sure you are:

- **CLEAR**: Are your energy signals confusing? Do you know what's in your heart? Be honest, nonjudgmental, accepting, and realistic in your assessment. You cannot raise your vibrational energy if your actions are in misalignment with your heart.

- **CONSISTENT**: Focus on what's important.

- **ATTUNED**: Review your timing and assess your energy levels.

- **PATIENT AND BELIEVING**: Magic (or the Universe) won't be hurried.

- **PRESENT**: Acknowledge what's around you and cultivate a grateful heart as you work toward your desired goals.

- **TRUSTING**: Trust that what's meant for you will manifest at the time you need it most.

- **KIND TO YOURSELF**: Engage in mindful meditation (see page 54), chakra work (see page 63), or other self-care rituals that make you feel like the magical being you are. Forgive yourself and others.

ALIGNING COLOR ENERGY WITH CRYSTAL ENERGY

Once intentions are set, selecting crystals based on the aligned energies—or your intuition—to include in your spellwork and rituals is the next step. Understand, too, that crystals and the abundance of colors in which they present can help you double down on their energetic vibrations for manifesting intentions.

Following is a list of colors and what their innate vibrational energies support as well as crystal suggestions to enhance working with these colors to realize your intentions. For a multi-boost from single stones, think crystals with multiple colors, like labradorite or even turquoise or opal. These stones carry the energies of all their colors combined.

Because colors are frequently assigned different or multiple meanings, and we all have our own memories and associations with color throughout life, experiment, have fun, and stay in tune with your intuition. Use the colors and crystals that feel right or speak to you. Look within to see your real magic.

BLACK

Detoxifying, grounding, powerful healing, protection, security, support in grief
Suggested crystals: black onyx, black tourmaline, obsidian

BLUE

Calm, healing, health, kindness, meditation, patience, sincerity, tranquility
Suggested crystals: aquamarine, lapis lazuli, sapphire

BRIGHT ORANGE

Happiness
Suggested crystals: orange calcite, peach selenite

BRIGHT PINK

Creativity, glamour
Suggested crystals: pink sapphire, rhodochrosite

BRONZE/BROWN

Clarity of thought, common sense, detoxifying, experience, grounding, longevity, prosperity, stability, strength
Suggested crystals: leopardskin jasper, smoky quartz

DARK BLUE

Peace, spirituality, tranquility
Suggested crystals: iolite

GOLD

Attraction, balance, creativity, changing luck, elegance, energy, fertility, joy, prestige, prosperity, success
Suggested crystals: golden apatite, pyrite, tiger's eye, topaz

GREEN

Abundance, children, Earth, feeling grounded, fertility, friendship, good luck, growth, healing, money, Nature, renewal, success, wealth
Suggested crystals: emerald, jade, moldavite, peridot

LAVENDER

Intuition, peace, protection, spiritual growth
Suggested crystals: lavender jade, tanzanite

ORANGE

Ambition, attraction, building energy, changing luck, courage, creativity, emotional healing, health, individuality, joy, personal power, warmth
Suggested crystals: carnelian, tiger's eye

PINK

Calm, clairvoyance, compassion, faith, friendship, harmony, joy, forgiveness, tenderness
Suggested crystals: pink opal, pink tourmaline, rose quartz

PURPLE

Authority, intuition, prosperity, spiritual
awareness, stress reduction, success,
wealth, wisdom
Suggested crystals: amethyst, tanzanite

RED/DEEP RED

Courage, motivation, passion, power, protection,
romantic love, security, vitality
Suggested crystals: garnet, red jasper

SILVER/GRAY

Clairvoyance, cleansing, healing, moonlight,
peace, rest, sophistication, truth
Suggested crystals: galena, silver banded agate,
silver topaz

TURQUOISE

Awakening, awareness, enlightenment
Suggested crystals: turquoise

VIOLET

Creativity, dreams, healing intuition,
psychic powers
Suggested crystals: amethyst, iolite, tanzanite

WHITE

Clairvoyance, cleansing, peace, protection, security, truth; white can also stand in for any color you want but don't have. Simply visualize the desired color as you light a white candle and take a moment to imagine the outcome you wish.
Suggested crystals: clear quartz, diamond, Herkimer diamond, moonstone, selenite

YELLOW

Balance, communication, confidence, creativity, happiness, intuition, joy, mental clarity, optimism, personal power and self-esteem, realizing and manifesting thoughts, success in business, warmth
Suggested crystals: citrine

Along with the crystals' colors, add colored candles, wear colored clothing (or makeup), drape your altar in color, or use the colors in Nature to connect as many energies as you can for positive outcomes.

CRYSTAL CLEANSING
AND ACTIVATION

After setting your intentions and selecting your crystals (or did they choose you?), it's likely you want to get right to work with them. There are a couple of key steps, however, that you need to take to make sure the crystals are ready to do the work you assign to them for the most successful outcomes.

When first bringing crystals home, or after working with them for a while, you will want to cleanse them to clear any negative energy they may contain—or have picked up by handling from others—and rebalance their vibrational energies. Note, too, that in addition to the methods noted here, you can also cleanse crystals in the Sun's magical light, but know that it can fade many of them, so do some research before using the Sun to cleanse and activate any crystals.

There is no rule for how often to cleanse, or reset, crystals, except when first working with them. A good general guideline is to cleanse your crystals once the intention you've imbued them with has manifested, or when setting new intentions. If you work with the Moon's magical cycle when setting intentions, that's about once a month. Or consider cleansing your crystals if they are in a room where someone has been ill or an argument has taken place, or when handled by others who may have disrupted their natural energy.

Some say that certain crystals, such as selenite, citrine, and clear quartz, do not need to be cleansed, and can even cleanse other crystals. The more you use your crystals, the more in tune you will be with when—or whether—a cleanse is in order. Let your intuition guide you. Following are some suggestions for ways to cleanse and activate your crystals, and by spending this bit of extra time with them, you'll get a sense of their energy and they of yours. As always, find something that speaks to you and enhances your magical vibrations. You and your crystals will shine brighter for it.

MOONLIGHT CLEANSE

Any crystal, and especially crystals that are not safe in water, can be cleansed and activated with the Moon's energetic glow. The Full Moon is an especially good time. Simply place your crystal somewhere it'll receive the Moon's light and leave it to bathe overnight to clear any negative energies and absorb her most potent power. It'll be activated and ready to absorb your intentions fully.

WATER CLEANSE

Although all quartz crystals are good candidates for a water cleanse, not all crystals take to water safely. If the crystal is water resistant, usually rated 7 or higher on the Mohs hardness scale, a simple dip in a cool water bath can be enough to cleanse it, or a more mindful rinse under running water while visualizing any negativity flowing away can be a powerful mini ritual. Add a pinch of Himalayan salt for a cleansing boost, if it is safe to do so (see following).

SALT CLEANSE

Salt is another tool used to cleanse and ready crystals for their important work. Like water, salt is not friendly to all crystals, so do your research. Typically, porous crystals, crystals that contain iron, or those that contain water are not good candidates for this method. Create a bed of salt (kosher, table, or sea salt), about 2 inches (5 cm) thick, in a bowl or other container that is large enough to hold your crystals. Lay them in the salt, and let cleanse for at least 30 minutes, or overnight. The salt draws out the negativity, leaving you with a clean slate on which to record your intentions.

If this method speaks to you but you're unsure about your crystals' suitability, place the crystals you wish to cleanse into a glass bowl, and set that bowl into the salt!

Do not reuse the salt after cleansing crystals in it. If you can, safely return it to Earth, with a nod of thanks for its gifts, or dispose of it another way, such as intentionally washing the negativity it contains down the drain, or place it in the trash, if you must.

◆ EARTH CLEANSE ◆

Returning your crystals to their place of birth is an energetically powerful way to cleanse and recharge them. Ensure the spot is safe and the location is marked and simply bury the crystals in Earth. If you live in a city without easy access to a safe spot to do this, a flowerpot filled with clean soil can stand in mightily for the same results. Any amount of time is sufficient to recalibrate the stone's vibrational energy; overnight under a Full Moon is ideal. If you plan to leave your crystals buried for a longer period of time, say, as a sort of time capsule, make sure you write down the location or you're likely to forget when the time comes to unearth your special treasure. Clean away any debris after you dig it up and take a moment to honor Earth for all she provides.

SMOKE CLEANSE

Smoke has the power to clear the air of unwanted vibes and harmful energies. It can do the same for your crystals. And though sage may be the traditional herb that comes to mind for smoke cleansing, really any herb that you like can be used. Rosemary, lavender, sandalwood, and cedar are all appropriate options for cleansing crystals. Simply—and safely—burn the herbs in a fireproof container and either wave the smoke over the crystals or pass the crystals through the smoke. While you have the cleansing fires lit, waft the smoke into the corners of the room and doorway to rid it of unwanted energies as well. Feel the negativity evaporating in the mist. Your crystals will now be ready to receive your energies and intentions.

VIBRATIONAL CLEANSE

The vibrations of sound are powerful cleansing allies in a magical environment and can cleanse your crystals, too. Get creative and have fun with this. Simple rituals can include the sound of your voice in chant or song passing over the crystals. Strike a gong, ring a chime, play a crystal or brass singing bowl, or play your favorite music. Use whatever vibrational sound is pleasing to you, and visualize the sound waves carrying the crystal's negative energies away like the breeze.

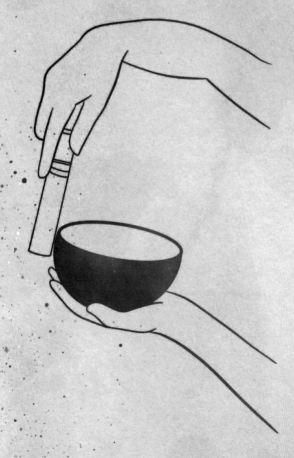

PROGRAMMING CRYSTALS
WITH INTENTIONS

Although crystals continue to vibrate their unique energies when not programmed, scripting them with our intentions ensures they vibrate to attract, or repel, or remind us of the very things we're working to manifest in our lives. It attunes them to your intentions and informs the work they do on your behalf, working in partnership, in harmony, to accomplish your goals.

Programming crystals is easy and based solely on your intentions. Once they are set (see page 20), it's time to bring the magic of crystal energies into the equation. Find a time you can be fully focused and relaxed. Breathe fully in and out, slowly, intentionally, as you feel yourself becoming fully grounded. Focus on your intention until it is clearly and specifically formed in your thoughts. Write it in your journal, if you wish.

Now, holding the crystal you've chosen to help manifest your intention, repeat your intention quietly or aloud, three times, or until you feel your crystal is filled with its energies. Visualize it being fulfilled. Take a moment in gratitude for the opportunity you have to manifest your magical life and for the crystal's work.

Place the crystal anywhere you feel will support your work: near your bed if your intention is monitoring and learning from dreams; in your office, if creativity at work is your goal; in a family space, if family harmony is on the agenda; or on your altar, where you'll see it daily as a reminder. You can also incorporate essential oils, candles, herbs, flowers, favorite goddesses, or any other element you may add to your rituals here. Use what complements and furthers your goals. Nothing is off-limits and your creativity rules the process.

As you work to achieve that which you have set in motion by releasing your thoughts and energies into the Universe, carry the crystal with you, if it makes sense, or touch base with it regularly to keep the energy active and flowing. Meditating with your crystal every day, even if just long enough to restate and refocus your intention, can bring powerful change to your life.

It's important to note that you are not "transferring" the intention work to the crystal alone, but aligning and anchoring vibrational energies to work in synergy to achieve your goals. You must continue to do the work needed to further and complete the process, monitoring and adjusting as needed. You have the power within to achieve that which your heart desires by choosing to believe it is your destiny and working to attract it into your life. Like attracts like, so choosing love in all your actions and intentions, for example, will attract more love to you. Same for any intentional energy you wish to manifest. Crystal energies amplify the message that you want broadcast to the Universe.

When you successfully manifest your intentions, be thankful for the gifts you've been given, then cleanse and reactivate your crystal allies as intentions grow and change.

STORING CRYSTALS

Your hardworking crystals deserve your care and protection to keep them clean, damage-free, and in tip-top shape. Some people prefer to keep crystals out and about, working and manifesting, where their energies as well as their beauty inspire life. Worn, or used in any room of the house (or office if you work outside of the house), crystals can help direct energies, offer protection, decorate, and delight. Regular light dusting and a thorough energy cleanse, when needed or when about to be put to use, will keep them vibrating happily. If you prefer this approach, do keep them out of direct sunlight, which can fade their beauty and energy.

Others prefer to store crystals when not in use, or to keep them away from curious kids and pets. If that's your preference, keep them in a safe place to prevent damage or dust collection—energetic, cosmic, or otherwise. Individually wrap delicate crystals in soft cloths, enclose them in their original packaging, or gently tuck them, wrapped, into a padded or lined box (like a jewelry box or a larger wooden box). Keeping crystals in closed display cases can also give you the best of both options.

Whatever you decide, keeping crystals near at hand and easily accessible when needed will ensure your magical life continues to flow uninterrupted. When you're ready to put your crystals into action again, a cleanse and reprogramming with your intentions will rekindle the magic.

Manifesting Magic

Crystals are an amazingly powerful tool you can use to complement, amplify, resonate, and direct energies to manifest your magical goals and are a natural complement to other healing practices you may incorporate into your magical life. As with all things magic, harnessing energy to release intentions means first having those intentions set (see page 20). Remember, too, that you'll see the strongest shifts in energy when focusing on one particular goal or theme—like, maybe, being more creative, which can help you be more successful—instead of multiple goals—like boosting creativity, finding a new job, and finding new love all at once (but if that's what you really need, then do what feels right!). Try not to spread yourself and your creative energies too thin for best results and to keep the focus on what's really important to you.

LET YOUR CRYSTAL MAGIC SHINE

C rystals can be incorporated into your magical workings however feels natural to you. They give us a rainbow of options to use within our magical lives and they're easy and portable enough to use on a daily basis. Simply adorn yourself with them to start, just because they make you feel better, and let your inner sparkle out! In addition to manifesting beauty, consider these other ways you can use crystals to conjure magic in your life, or use these suggestions as a starting point to develop your own rituals.

- Add crystals to your **meditative work** (see page 56) to define and confirm intentions, connect with your intuition, bring peace and harmony to your day, work on goals and affirmations, or ease the transition from busy day to silent night.

- Add crystal magic to your **journaling** sessions (see page 58) to help ground your thoughts for clarity or take them to the heavens for a chat with your spiritual guides.

- Keep your mind, body, and spirit aligned and your vital energies flowing by incorporating crystals into **chakra meditation** (see page 142).

- **Decorate your altar** based on intentions or add crystals to amplify the energies you've set there, using their color, inherent message, or ability to enhance the energies around it to support your work (see page 51).

- Match crystal energy to a **ritual bath** (see page 152). Whether for healing, calming, energizing, beautifying, tantalizing, mesmerizing, abundance, compassion, sweet sleep, or just because, there is a crystal to enhance your life and purpose. Bury a (salt-safe) crystal based on intention into homemade or store-bought bath salts to infuse the salts with energy before adding them to your bath. Do take care that any crystals added to a bath are water resistant.

- Place crystals in your **garden** to attract fae friends or support your plants' lush growth.

- **Carry in your car or luggage** for safe travel vibes.

- Brew **crystal elixirs.** (Always know the stones you're working with. Some are not water-safe and some can be harmful and even toxic.)

- Use as **offerings** to goddesses, fairies, or other magical beings you call upon for help and guidance.

- Incorporate crystals into **spellwork** for the extra boost of energy.

- Add crystals to your **Moon magic** spells and rituals (see page 48).

- **Adorn yourself** with your favorite crystals, or carry them in a pocket, pouch, purse, or wallet, because every magical life needs a little beauty and indulgence to shine its brightest sometimes.

- Create a **crystal grid** (see page 72).

- Make a **magic wand** to activate your crystal grid.

- Try **crystal scrying** (see page 44) to connect with messages divine in nature.

- Purposefully **place crystals around your home or office**, using feng shui principles, if you like, or place them intuitively based on what you think looks and feels good, to invite specific energies in or keep specific energies out, such as one under the bed to incite a little romance or under your pillow for dreams, whether sweet or clairvoyant, or to ward off nightmares.

- Add to **spell jars** and **poppets**.

- Simply **enjoy their natural beauty** while they work their magic on your behalf.

- Give crystals as **gifts** and pay the magic forward.

SHIMMERING BEAUTY

Another fun—and effective—way to incorporate crystals into your everyday rituals is to include them in your beauty routine. Along with their intrinsic energetic properties, crystals' gorgeous colors and shimmery appeal have found their way into all manner of beauty products intended to bring out your inner glow and polish that outer sparkle. From facial rollers to eye shadows, facial mists and hydrating elixirs, face creams, cleansers, body scrubs, soaps, bath soaks, crystal-infused essential oils, fragrances, and more, radiance is guaranteed. Bonus: Many of these products are made with great care for Earth, giver of these crystal beauties, and great care for you, with organic, sustainable, and ethically sourced materials intended to nourish and pamper.

CRYSTAL SCRYING

Also called crystal gazing, scrying, in general, is an act of divination, a process by which one seeks to foretell the future by staring into a reflective surface looking for images or visions that hint at things to come or things that may have been. Scrying has been practiced for thousands of years by peoples of numerous cultures and may be the first thing you think of when beginning to incorporate crystals into your magical life. You may use crystal scrying to receive messages from the Universe, seek the help and wisdom of your spirit, for healing, to delve into the past, see more clearly into the present, or predict what the future holds, among other things.

Among the many tools used for this form of divination are the oft-gazed crystal ball as well as other reflective objects, such as mirrors, candle flames, and water. Of course, crystal scrying uses crystals as the reflective medium. Clear crystals, such as clear quartz or amethyst, or dark polished stones, such as labradorite, obsidian, or tiger's eye, are the best to choose for scrying. Use crystal balls, skulls, or other shapes that are highly reflective and, thus, able to suggest images, or hints of images, for you to interpret. As always, choose a crystal for scrying that resonates deeply with you. Think of crystal gazing as a partnership—it is you who has the ability to see, and the crystal is there to support you with its energy and as a tool for you to focus your mind. You may also choose the type of crystal based on its energy or your intention, as with your other crystal magic work.

As in meditation, where you strive to clear the mind of clutter by focusing on your breathing or a particular sound to provide the unconscious room to expand, the same principle is at work here. Relax. Do not force anything. There is no room for judgment here. You want your psychic eye—third eye—to open and see what the physical eyes cannot. Give your intuition over to receiving the messages it's meant to hear.

CRYSTAL GAZING BASICS

As you begin to explore crystal gazing, remember to approach it with a true heart and understand that results may not happen instantly. Don't give up on your magic. It's there, just waiting to be called to action. Your sessions do not have to be elaborate or wrapped in ritual unless that is your preference.

To prepare for a successful scrying session, select a quiet place when you have time to spend and will not be disturbed. Nighttime is frequently suggested for its connection to the intuitive mind. Once you've selected your crystal, it needs to be cleansed—a simple smoke cleansing can work, or you may leave it under the Moon's light before scrying (the Full Moon is best for this).

1. Place the crystal somewhere you can sit comfortably with it—a quiet location with soft lighting is ideal—for 10 to 20 minutes.

2. Light a candle or two, if you desire, and position the candles so the light is not reflecting directly off the crystal's surface.

3. Take a minute to center yourself and acknowledge the problem or intention before you, as you ask for guidance and answers. Breathe in fully, visualizing yourself being filled with a calming, soothing light, and breathe out fully, releasing any tensions and doubts, until you feel completely relaxed.

4. With a soft focus, gaze into your crystal. Focus your mind on the crystal and let it stay clear. If your mind wanders, acknowledge it and gently return your focus to the crystal. Be patient and stay relaxed, but be fully aware of any images, words, symbols, colors, sounds, emotions, or sensations that may come to you.

5. Continue to gaze into the crystal, keeping a clear mind and a soft focus. Images may continue to come to you, or your intuition may speak. Tapping deep into the well of your subconscious, intuitive mind takes practice. Don't be discouraged if you're unsure of the results immediately.

6. When finished, close your eyes, breathe deeply in and out, and feel your physical body in touch with its surroundings.

7. Take a moment to thank the Universe or your spirit guides for their help, protection, and wisdom. Reflect on the messages received, then record them in your journal, even if they're not clear to you yet or seem incomplete. You may intuitively know their meaning immediately, or you may need to meditate or journal on the messages to gain their full significance. Stay alert for other messages that may come to you in dreams, or in coincidences after your scrying session.

8. Store your scrying crystal respectfully until you're ready to try again.

Remember, the answers are wisely within you . . . the crystal gently reflects what's in your heart so you may see its messages more clearly.

CRYSTAL MAGIC ✦ MOON MAGIC

Think of it: The Moon is just one large crystal in the sky—and, oh, her powerful energies, available to anyone who asks, can be combined with other crystal energies for some stellar magical workings. And, unlike other crystals whose energies remain constant, the Moon's changing phases mean her energies wax and wane over the course of her monthly journey through our skies. Attuning to those energies and incorporating crystals to magnify, align, or, perhaps, even tame, can be a forceful combination for manifesting intentions.

NEW MOON

Active phase; time to set intentions; new beginnings; new resolutions

Choose crystals aligned with new ideas and beginnings, such as amazonite, beryl, chrysocolla, clear quartz, green jade, labradorite, or tiger's eye.

WAXING CRESCENT

Reflective phase; refine intentions and consider actions needed to manifest them

Choose crystals aligned with motivation and courage to support change, such as carnelian, garnet, or rose quartz.

FIRST QUARTER

Active phase; take appropriate actions to realize intentions as energies build

Choose crystals aligned with empowering energies, such as aquamarine, pyrite, red jasper, or sunstone.

WAXING GIBBOUS

Reflective phase; trust that your actions are aligned with your intentions

Choose crystals aligned with staying grounded and positive as well as adapting to change, such as citrine, rainbow moonstone, tiger's eye, or turquoise.

FULL MOON

Active phase; assess results, celebrate achievements, and offer gratitude for your abundance; also a time of letting go

Choose crystals aligned with high energy and manifestation, such as clear quartz, green aventurine, moldavite, moonstone, or selenite.

WANING GIBBOUS

Reflective phase; assess progress and lessons learned, request feedback, share your story; recognize what no longer serves

Choose crystals aligned with gratitude and easing stress, such as amethyst, angelite, black tourmaline, or sapphire.

LAST (THIRD) QUARTER

Active phase; let go of anything that is not a positive force in your life; indulge in self-care to recharge batteries; forgiveness

Choose crystals aligned with knowing when to let go, so new ideas and growth emerge, such as blue lace agate, malachite, or obsidian.

WANING CRESCENT

Reflective phase; rest, appreciate the quiet so you can hear your soul talking as you prepare to set new intentions

Choose crystals aligned with rest, reflection, and self-compassion, such as bloodstone, pink tourmaline, prehnite, or rose quartz.

CREATING A CRYSTAL ALTAR

Having an altar as a dedicated magical space for you to work is optional, but a dedicated crystal altar can be a fun space to create and use in your magical practice to inspire your work. An altar defines your sacred space and provides a visual reminder and a physical presence—inside or outside, when working in groups or alone—to focus your energy, meditate, or try a crystal spell or two. It can serve as one place to display crystals you're currently working with or to create a crystal grid (see page 72); it can be dedicated to specific intentions as they manifest and change, or you can incorporate crystals into other altars you may have, such as one dedicated to the Moon, goddesses, fairies, Mother Nature, or your ancestors . . . whatever approach feels right is how you should proceed, and that may change over time.

Your altar does not have to be fancy and can be as simple as a windowsill or cardboard box. It can even be a shelf or tabletop where you display your crystals, candles, tarot cards, or other reminders of your intentions and priorities, to keep you aware every day of the work you're doing. It honors your intentions and the importance they have in your life. You may even decide to have more than one altar—one inside and one outside to celebrate Nature's beauty, changing with the seasons, honoring Nature and your life's intentions as they grow and evolve.

You can also create altars reflecting specific intentions: Set up an altar in your bedroom devoted to romance; one in a quiet corner for cultivating gratitude or gathering strength; even in the bathroom for cleansing and renewing rituals. Be as fancy, creative, or minimalist as you like. Your altar represents you— your heart, hopes, dreams, intentions, and life. If you stay true to your heart, your altar will be ready to help you work your magic when called upon.

— DECORATING YOUR CRYSTAL ALTAR —

Decorating your altar is a personal choice. Cover your altar with a cloth, if you wish—maybe in a color that represents your intentions. As much as possible, keep the elements that make up your altar natural, for their innate individual energies.

Before decorating, physically cleaning the space where your altar resides removes negative energy and makes room for good vibes to flourish. Wipe it clean with rosemary water or rose water. Sweep it clean with a bundle of lavender blooms. Ceremonially cleansing your space can be an alternative. Consider a besom broom or common sage cleansing spray or smoke cleanse to help whisk away any energy that does not serve.

On your altar, you may wish to include any or all of the following, but always do what feels right to you and is true to your heart:

- Your favorite crystals that you share a special connection with (always) in addition to the crystals whose vibrational energies support your goals and intentions (which will change).

- Scrying crystals for divination work.

- Clean water, whether imbued with energy from a chosen (water-safe) crystal, charged by the Full Moon's light, or sourced from a river, stream, or ocean, for cleansing and blessing your altar.

- A bowl of clean soil, Himalayan salt, or seeds to represent the element of Earth and all you appreciate of her gifts and ability to grow the magnificent crystals in your life.

- Candles in colors that support your intentions, or use colored crystal candleholders with white candles in their place.

- A crystal wand crafted from a found twig or branch that crossed your path to activate your crystal grid (see page 72) or use in spellwork.

- Essential oils to incorporate into spellwork or rituals, or for use in meditation.

- Pictures of loved ones, or other reminders of those important to you.

- Crystal tarot cards, rune tiles, a small cauldron, or other tools to assist in daily meditation, intention setting, or spellwork.

- Dried herbs, fresh flowers, or other plants to reflect your intentions and add an element of natural beauty to celebrate and magnify the energies your soul seeks.

- Books that have special meaning, including a journal.

- Bells, chimes, or singing bowl to center the mind and use to cleanse your crystals.

- A mini wishing well to collect your crystal wishes.

- Found things—they're gifts from the Universe.

MINDFUL MEDITATION

Another useful tool in harnessing crystal energy is mindful meditation. This type of meditation offers the chance to slow down and reflect, to fill the crystals with your intentions and refill your energy reservoir with their vibrations, while exploring your heart, priorities, and goals. Incorporating crystals into your meditative practice gives you a tangible item to focus on and can deepen your meditative state.

To meditate, in general, is to engage in contemplation or reflection, or to engage in a mental exercise (as in concentrating on your breathing or repeating a mantra) to reach a heightened level of spiritual awareness. Buddhists, who have been practicing meditation for millennia, believe it develops concentration, clarity, emotional positivity, and a calmness that is needed to see the truth. When you focus your thoughts, you eliminate the endless lists running through your brain that may be causing you stress or worry, or that are making it hard to focus and make decisions.

Mindful meditation is the practice of being present, where you strive for an increased awareness of being in the moment, *without preconceived notions or judgment*, and paying attention to yourself—your breathing, emotions, sensations, and thoughts. Meditation is not about tuning out everything in our lives but, rather, tuning in to the present and being with ourselves.

For those who practice meditation, it is commonly a way to relieve stress and reduce anxiety. If you've been meditating for a while, you have already experienced the positive things it can bring to your life. If not, you have nothing to lose; there is no right or wrong, and it doesn't have to take a lot of time.

Regular meditation can bring about a transforming sense of relaxation and ease. Learning to focus your thoughts helps clear the clutter that can accumulate in our brains. It helps us see what matters most and, more importantly, just *be* for a while. Meditation has been said to contribute to overall improved physical and mental well-being, including helping develop a new perspective on stressful situations, reducing negative emotions and reactions, boosting creativity, fostering acceptance, decreasing pain, and increasing happiness. Meditation can also help develop your intuitive senses, which are helpful for all your magical work.

You don't need a lot of, or really any, fancy equipment or gear to meditate—only a quiet space (outdoors surrounded by Nature is a great option), a crystal, a comfortable position, and an open mind. Make this as fancy as you like or as simple as just breathing.

Mindful meditation takes practice and consistency—even 10 minutes a day as part of your self-care regimen can help—but once you begin to feel the benefits in your life, you will crave the quiet peace that meditation affords. Whatever you choose to make it, make it regular and stress-free.

CRYSTAL MEDITATION BASICS

ind a quiet, comfortable place where you won't be disturbed. Relax. Set a gentle alarm, if you wish to time your session.

Choose and cleanse. Choose the crystal whose energy you wish to use and release into the Universe. Cleanse the crystal (see page 28), if you feel it's needed before you begin. Gently holding the crystal in your hands, feel its shape, weight, warmth or coolness, texture, and energy. Absorb its color energy. Visualize the crystal's energy flowing into you and your energy and intentions flowing into the crystal as a continual process, like breathing in and breathing out. Ask the crystal to help. How do you feel? What messages might you be receiving?

Close your eyes, if you are comfortable doing so, to limit visual distractions.

Breathe. Bring your attention to your breathing. Breathe in and out through your nose, naturally, yet fully. Focus your attention on each in-breath and out-breath; feel your body grow on the in-breath and feel it collapse on the out-breath. Feel your breath calming and centering the energy within you—let yourself relax.

Imagine each inhale fills you with crystal sparkle and wisdom—from top to bottom—cleansing and clearing any negativity, hurt, or fear.

Visualize your exhale taking with it anything causing you pain, as you replace it on the inhale with soothing kindness and infinite power.

Focus. As you concentrate on your breath, your mind may wander. Gently acknowledge it and return your focus to your breath. Listen to your soul. Has it really been heard lately? Alternatively, as you continue your breathing, you may scan your body, focusing your attention solely on one part before moving on to the next, starting at your toes and moving upward to your scalp. If a particular body part feels tense or painful, focus your mind, breathing, and crystal healing energy on that part until it is relaxed, then move on to the next. Place the crystal there, if it helps. Again, if your attention wanders, gently refocus and continue the process.

Be grateful. When your timer sounds, or you are ready, return your focus to your surroundings. Open your eyes. Wiggle your toes. Feel the crystal in your hands. Take a moment to give thanks for the quiet time and be grateful for the space that welcomes you before returning to your normal activities, charged with crystal energy that both soothes and inspires.

Be attuned. Be attuned to the universal workings around you and the influence of the crystal's energy as you work toward your intentions. You may want to journal about your experiences, if it helps.

⌁ JOURNALING ⌁

Another way to manifest with crystal magic is through journaling. Whatever you desire to manifest, crystal energy can help you develop a deeper focus and connection to your thoughts and feelings. Then, putting your intentions into writing—whether in a diary, journal, calendar, or other volume—creates a record to serve as a reminder as well as one you can reflect on and check in on for progress along the way. Taking time to write down your thoughts and feelings is a chance to add some quiet to your life—to break away from the constant noise and busyness, and look, instead, into the hypnotic energies of your crystals and deep into your heart and mind to determine or remind yourself what matters.

Putting things in writing, too, moves you from the "thought" stage to the "action" stage. It keeps you committed, motivated, focused, reminded. It frees up space in your brain for other things. It keeps you grateful and honest. It can reduce stress. Writing about your dreams and intentions creates another form of energy to release your thoughts into the Universe. Crystals motivate and amplify those energies.

When journaling with crystals, you may want to sit with crystals that resonate energies aligned with specific issues or intentions, or select crystals intuitively. Let them choose you and let the crystal energy work through you, addressing everyday issues and concerns, in a way that feels most natural to you.

Note, too, your throat chakra, linked with the color blue, influences communication, including your ability to listen well and without judgment, express yourself, and have confidence in speaking your truth. Keep a blue crystal, such as angelite, aquamarine, blue kyanite, or sapphire, with your journal when not in use, and nearby when journaling to keep all the magical energies flowing smoothly.

Your journal is your safe space. There is no room for judgment here—only magical thinking and truth.

CRYSTAL JOURNALING TIPS

- ↜ Keep a crystal wish list or use your journal as a place to inventory your crystal collection as it grows and all you've learned about working with each crystal.

- ↜ Journal after meditating, especially when using crystals. What did you learn? What do you still need to know? What surprised you? Write about your inner needs and desires brought into clearer focus with crystal energy.

- ᖇ Decorate your journal with crystal drawings or images, affirmations, poetry, or spells that evoke your favorite crystal energies.

- ᖇ Write down questions you wish to explore with your crystals or record times you felt their energies working on your behalf, including where you were and what you were doing. Let your writing channel their messages.

- ᖇ Create affirmations that channel crystal energy and support your intentions.

- ᖇ Sketch ideas for crystal grids attuned to specific intentions.

- ᖇ Journal about crystal spells and rituals you've tried and created, and record their results or monitor their progress.

- ᖇ Record outcomes of chakra work and reflect on improvements it lends to your life.

- ᖇ Keep track of messages received when scrying and note related thoughts as they occur to you.

- ᖇ Log your dreams, especially when asking for crystal energy to receive messages from the Universe.

- ᖇ Incorporate gratitude into your journaling for all the positive influences you have access to in your life.

Journal daily or only as needed, but make space in your life to let the magic in. Don't be afraid to ask questions and write down your honest feelings and self-empowering thoughts. And above all, *notice the sense of peace and fulfillment you get when you align desires, thoughts, and actions—intentionally.*

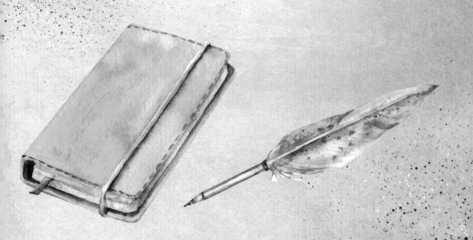

As you start your crystal magic journey, remember:

*Don't hide your spark. Let it help others light their path.
Acknowledge the spark in others.*

*Express gratitude for the magical life you have and
work hard to be true to yourself.*

*Honor the Earth for her crystal gifts and thank your
crystals for their illuminating presence in your life.*

*Believe in your beautiful magic.
It is unique to you but can touch many.*

Chakras, Crystal Grids & Sacred Geometry

In the way that crystals vibrate with innate energies born of the Earth and from the alignment of their molecules expressed uniquely in each one, so, too, do our body, mind, and spirit vibrate with unique inherent energies manifested by all living things. These energies, as chakras, are said to be aligned along the spine—from its base to the very top of your head—and provide the life force needed for your mind, spirit, and body to work at their very best.

Chakra means "wheel" in Sanskrit, and your seven major chakras, when unblocked and spinning unencumbered, with vital energies flowing freely in and out, are what keep your magical life turning in harmony. Chakras, when blocked or thrown off-balance by stress, anxiety, illness, or other emotional turmoil, can create physical, emotional, and spiritual problems as the energies become backed up or stagnant. Even one unbalanced chakra can affect the whole, like that kink in your bike chain that throws the whole system out of whack.

WORKING WITH CHAKRA ENERGY

Working with your chakras in your magical practice, just like incorporating the energies of herbs, crystals, or the Moon, allows you to consciously bring more ease, joy, spirituality, creativity, and success into your life—all reasons you work to manifest intentions in your magical practice. If a chakra is blocked, your magical energy is blocked, too. Keep every magical component at your disposal in top operating condition. Explore what feels right to you and learn as you go. There is no right or wrong way here, and the search for higher meaning in life can only bring you closer to your goals.

Color associations (see more on page 23) are important in all of our magical workings, and especially with crystals. Chakras, too, have color associations—those of the rainbow and its magical energies—that can be used to help you select crystals to align energies. You can also match crystals with intentions and associated chakra/color energy to tune up your system and effectively communicate your messages to the Universe.

Like the elements associated with Wicca and other Nature-based belief systems, the chakras are also associated with an element and provide another subtle connection to the Earth and Nature as we honor them and strive to connect in pursuit of our goals and a life filled with purpose. Keeping those energies working at optimal speed is an important part of the equation.

WHO IS ROY G. BIV?

The colors of a rainbow appear in a specific—dazzling—order, created when the colors comprising light are bent, or refracted, by, say, raindrops or a prism. To remember which order those colors present in the sky, let me introduce you to Roy G. Biv . . . this colorful chap can help you get them right every time: Red, Orange, Yellow, Green, Blue, Indigo, Violet!

UNDERSTANDING THE SEVEN MAJOR CHAKRAS

The first three chakras, beginning at the base of the spine, are more physical in nature, whereas the last three are more spiritual. The heart chakra, in the middle, is the bridge between the two areas. The crystal companions suggested here are just that, suggestions, a place to start. As with all your magical workings, use what speaks to you. If you find a particular crystal helpful for grounding work that's not listed here, go for it! Same for any intentions you wish to make real and any energies you wish to draw to you. Use what speaks to you and don't be afraid to try something new or different to get the results you desire.

ROOT, or *muladhara*: the main source of energy, located at the base of the spine; linked with the color red and the element Earth.

The root chakra is believed to establish your connection with the world. When balanced, you feel secure, grounded, positive, independent, and successful; when unbalanced, you're left with feelings of insecurity, fear, and frustration.

Magical workings: Use this chakra to focus your meditation work and your spellwork. A freely flowing root chakra opens you to a depth of self-knowledge you can use to manage your strengths and weaknesses to live the magical life you desire.

Crystal companions: black tourmaline, bloodstone, clear quartz, garnet, hematite, obsidian, red jasper, ruby, smoky quartz

SACRAL, or PELVIC, or *svadhisthana*: located just below the navel; linked with the color orange and the element water.

The sacral chakra's energies are associated with compassion, creativity, fertility, happiness, intuition, and sexuality. When balanced, ideas flow freely, emotions are stable, and change is easily navigated; when unbalanced, you may feel emotionally off-kilter, stagnant, and rigid.

Magical workings: This chakra opens your connection to others. Keep it in focus when working in groups for magical outcomes or when working alone on relationship-based intentions.

Crystal companions: carnelian, clear quartz, garnet, sunstone

SOLAR PLEXUS, or *manipura*: located between the navel and rib cage; linked with the color yellow and the element fire.

Sometimes referred to as our "second brain" (trust your gut!), the solar plexus is the energy center of self-esteem, self-control, ego, and associated emotions. When balanced, you feel confident, passionate, productive, healthy, and happy; when unbalanced, you can be plagued with digestive issues and feel depressed, angry, generally unhappy, and insecure.

Magical workings: This chakra is your call to action in manifesting intentions. Keep it turning freely for your most magical results.

Crystal companions: amber, citrine, clear quartz, moonstone, tiger's eye

HEART, or *anahata*: located at the center of the cardiovascular system; linked to the color green and the element air.

The heart chakra joins the higher chakras in the body to the lower ones. It is connected to the emotions of the heart—love and self-love, trust, passion, forgiveness, and compassion. When balanced, life is calm and good and you feel lucky; when unbalanced, jealousy, loneliness, and fear rule and blood pressure soars.

Magical workings: The heart chakra, in its most balanced mode, will help with all manner of love spells, whether for yourself, the world, a friend or family member, all of Nature's creations, or a lover. You can give as well as receive love freely.

Crystal companions: aventurine, clear quartz, emerald, green jade, green tourmaline, malachite, rose quartz, ruby

THROAT, or *vishuddha*: located (obviously) in the throat; linked with the color blue and the element ether.

Believed to govern all associated areas of the throat, this chakra influences communication, including your ability to listen well and without judgment, express yourself, and have confidence in speaking your truth. When balanced, communication is clear, heartfelt, honest, and positive—you feel heard and understood and you hear others and your own intuition speaking; when unbalanced, you may have a hard time connecting your words to your emotions and beliefs, speak negatively of others, or talk too much without listening enough.

Magical workings: Keep your journaling on point, your intentions clear, and your spellwork articulate and working like a charm with a well-tuned throat chakra.

Crystal companions: amazonite, angelite, aquamarine, blue kyanite, blue lace agate, blue topaz, clear quartz, lapis lazuli, opal, turquoise

THIRD EYE, or *ajna*: located in the center of your forehead; linked with the color indigo and the element of light.

Governing your intellect and associated abilities such as intuition and the ability to see what may not be right in front of you, the third eye sees beyond the physical world and enables you to connect with its unseen wisdom. When balanced, you'll feel unencumbered, trusting of your instincts, and connected to a higher purpose—you see clearly; when unbalanced, you may experience headaches and feel aimless and closed-minded.

Magical workings: When your witchy intuition seems to be out of order, check in with this chakra. When it's working properly, you'll feel the vibrations of the world around you in harmony with your own.

Crystal companions: celestite, clear quartz, labradorite, lapis lazuli, moldavite, sapphire

CROWN, or *sahastrara*: located at the top of your head, this highest of chakras is linked with the colors purple and white and the element of cosmic energy.

This energy center controls thought, wisdom, enlightenment, and self-knowledge. When balanced, you feel beautiful and connected to everything and everyone, living a mindful existence; when unbalanced, you may experience confusion, a lack of focus, and a lack of connection to the things around you—you look for happiness outside versus in.

Magical workings: When you're ready to try a little magic beyond your physical realm, tune in to the energies of your crown chakra.

Crystal companions: amethyst, clear quartz, selenite, tanzanite

CRYSTAL GRIDS AND SACRED GEOMETRY

If you're new to crystal work, you may be unfamiliar with crystal grids. These grids, considered advanced crystal work, can seem complicated, but are simply another way to use crystals to amplify energies and manifest intentions. They're an energy pathway just like your chakras (see page 63). And because they are a little more work than just meditating with a single crystal, wearing crystals, or indulging in a crystal bath, crystal grids can be useful for those longer-term goals you're working on—but don't let that limit how you use them. Crystal grids are here for you when you need them.

Crystal grids are a purposeful, typically symmetrical, arrangement of crystals (whose energies represent your intentions) and form sacred geometrical shapes (or, really, any shape that speaks to you or has significance). The shape itself then contributes its inherent meanings and energies to the equation.

And because true crystals are the personification of sacred geometry (see page 74) in their perfectly repeating patterns of shapes, they are uniquely suited to this type of magical energy work where they are extremely powerful when combined in this fashion.

Crystal grids can be used for healing, abundance, creativity, success, love, compassion, friendship, protection, or any intention you wish to make real, or to conjure specific energies into your life. It's the alignment, synergies, and amplifications of the energies in the crystals, in your intentions, in the grid's shape, and *in the Universe* that boost the crystals' magic into high gear. Don't be intimidated by crystal grids. There are lots of online resources for templates to follow, or create your own. You can't get it wrong and the payoff can be big! Start small and let your grids grow along with your intention-filled life.

SACRED GEOMETRY

The concept of sacred geometry traces its ancient roots to the belief that God, as architect of the Universe, created everything with intent and a plan. Sacred geometry formations exist everywhere in Nature and their patterns are spoken in the language of mathematics. It is the explanation for how all of Nature organizes itself and is based on repeating geometric patterns; it is the energy that is all creation, its origins and unification.

Sacred geometry connects us more closely to the Universe and her energies. Contemplation of the sacred codes—shapes—allows us to think more deeply about the meanings of the objects that populate our world and that have significance to us.

The circle is a perfect example. As a symbol, a circle can represent the life cycle, eternity, perfection, safety, and the Universe. Reaching back to the spiraling chaos that was the beginning of time, circles exist everywhere in Nature. Some examples include the Earth and Moon, Saturn's rings, a tree's rings, the iris of your eye, ripples in a pond, the seed head of a sunflower, the eye of a hurricane, and our fingerprints. It is this connection with Nature that is honored by the sacred circle in the tradition of Wicca. The circle is cast to harness and contain positive energy and keep out negative energy, forming an energetic sacred space of safety and protection. Other sacred forms have other meanings, such as:

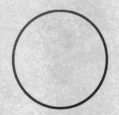

CIRCLE (SPHERE)

Perhaps the shape that started it all; continuity, harmony, protection, universal cycles

CROSS

Intersection of heaven and Earth

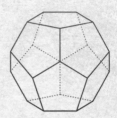

DODECAHEDRON

Spirit element; intuition

FLOWER OF LIFE

Universal depiction of the connection of all living things

ICOSAHEDRON

Water element; ease, change

MERKABA (3D STAR)

Light, spirit, body; sacred truth

OCTAHEDRON

Air element; kindness, compassion, love

SEED OF LIFE

Blessing and protection

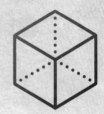

SPIRAL

Flow of energy; as above, so below

SQUARE

Stability; as a cube, the Earth element

TETRAHEDRON (PYRAMID)

Fire element; harmony, balance

Crystals cut into these, and other, sacred geometric shapes (as is practical) carry double the power: that of the stone and that of the shape. Choose wisely, or let your intuition guide you.

CRYSTAL GRID BASICS

Really look at your crystals to see their unique beauty. What patterns do you see? How can those naturally occurring patterns support your intentions and complement the crystal's energy? Are some patterns more soothing to you than others? Use that magical intuition to home in on what your spirit, body, or soul needs.

Although there is a typical formula, or arrangement, for creating crystal grids, as with all your magical workings, follow your heart and your intuition. (Don't worry: There is no need for a compass, protractor, or slide rule here!) Grids can be simple shapes, interlocking forms, concentric shapes, or repeating patterns. The ideas are limitless. However, if free-form feels right to you today, create with those energies. If patterned and traditional feels right, go with that. You can create your own shape or find any number of ideas or templates online to recreate.

CRYSTAL GRID SETUP AND ACTIVATION

The first step in creating a crystal grid is to know your intention. Whether this is something you've been meditating on for a while or just a gut feeling or pull to action you're experiencing, take a moment to close your eyes, if you're comfortable, center yourself and your breathing, and check in with your heart and intuition to make sure your intention is true and aligned with your purpose.

Choose a location, someplace your grid can remain undisturbed; your altar is a good place to start if you have one dedicated to your magical work. You may want to physically and/ or energetically cleanse the space before setting up your grid.

Select crystals that align with your intentions, including one to serve as a *center point* of your grid, which is typically the largest crystal, serving as the energy anchor. Think of it like your root chakra (see page 66). When choosing crystals, consider not only your intentions and how the crystals' energies align with them, but also their size, color, and shape as well as any intuitive connection you may have to other crystals you include. The additional stones you choose will surround the center point to create your chosen harmonizing, geometric pattern and the energy pathways of the grid. They serve to receive and clarify the energy of the center stone and your intentions. Cleanse the crystals you've chosen, if needed.

Holding your center point crystal, and whether visualizing or speaking aloud, state your intention for the grid to this center stone, imprinting the stone with it. Ask the crystal to hold your

WHICH WAY SHOULD I GO?

If your intentions concern drawing something to you, such as abundance, creativity, love, luck, friends, etc., activate your crystal grid in a clockwise direction.

If your intentions are to keep something away from you, such as negative energy or influences, or illness, or concern protection or letting go of something that no longer serves, activate your grid in a counterclockwise direction.

intention, then place it in your grid. Arrange the remaining crystals you've chosen to vibrate with your intentions around the center point in your chosen geometrical pattern.

To further amplify the grid's energies, place additional crystals, typically quartz crystals because of their strong vibrational properties, betwixt and between the surrounding stones of your grid.

Lastly, if it feels right to you, **place an object in your grid that represents your intentions.** Natural objects such as other stones, flowers, seeds, herbs, water, etc., carry the most energy, but you may also include photos, books, statues, poems, letters, candles (of course, do not leave lit candles unattended on your grid), or whatever most accurately represents your messages to the Universe.

To activate your crystal grid, hold your dominant hand over the center stone and feel the vibrations of your intentions. Slowly and deliberately, move your hand over each crystal you've placed in the grid to connect their energies to the center stone. You can also do this with a crystal wand (one you've built will have more of your energy). When the circuit feels complete to you, take a moment to acknowledge the work your crystals are doing for you and step back so they can do their work.

Leave your grid untouched for as long as you feel the energies flowing through it. It is good practice to spend some time with it, meditating or journaling on your intentions, as a sort of progress check-in and to see where adjustments in your actions toward manifesting your goals may be needed.

RECHARGING YOUR CRYSTAL GRID

If you feel like the grid needs a recharge, dismantle it, recharge the crystals under a Full Moon's light, if possible, cleanse the surface your grid rests on, dust off the crystals, and then reassemble the grid, recharging it with your intentions as you go.

If you're after a simpler recharge, take a few moments to center yourself and meditate on the intentions imbued in your crystal grid. When ready, gently blow your breath, carrying those intentions, over the grid. Take a moment to acknowledge the crystals for their work on your behalf.

FURTHER ENHANCING YOUR CRYSTAL GRID'S ENERGY

If you're so inclined, or your intentions really need a rocket booster to get them circulating into the Universe, consider creating your grid and manifesting your intentions aligned with the Moon's magical energies and phases (see page 48). Or use the days of the week correspondences or planetary correspondences to determine the best time to set up or recharge your grid.

Magical Crystal Jewel Box

W hat magic awaits as you lift the lid on your treasured jewel box? What sparkle catches your eye or energy grabs your heart? What memories of intentions manifested remind you of your power and what sparks of opportunity await their chance to shine?

Forty-six crystals lie ahead, just waiting for you to discover their power to transform all aspects of your magical life. Many are common and easy to source; others may be a bit more unusual, but are worth the effort to find, if their stories resonate with you. All are beautiful and all are magical. Will they call your name or will you choose them? Your beauty and magic complete the equation. Keep an open mind and a curious heart as you begin.

ETHICALLY SOURCED CRYSTALS

Crystals are Mother Earth's gift to us. They carry her spirit and energies and connect us to the universal wisdom embedded in their hearts during formation, over millions of years, in the quiet stillness of Earth's womb. In order for crystals to emerge from Earth clean, vibrating freely of negative energy, and able to heal us and manifest our highest good, we must care for their source, Earth, as well as for the people and processes that bring these crystals to us.

We are drawn to crystals by a life force greater than our own. Millions of others share our quest for joy and light, and our deep concern for Earth and her inhabitants. And, although it would be ideal to source crystals directly from Earth, in your patch of land, they typically come to us through a complicated and industrialized process, touched by many. Whether those who touch crystals care for them as we do is not always known, so buying from trusted sources who practice ethical, sustainable, fair, and safe harvesting—good for the planet and its people—is key. Similar to agriculture's farm-to-table movement, tracking the source and journey of your food until it reaches your table, crystals take a similar journey, but their origins can be difficult to track.

Options exist for doing your research in terms of crystal origins and knowing what you purchase, beyond that it calls to you or looks lovely. Options also exist for researching sellers with whom you can establish a trusted relationship (keeping in mind they, too, rely on others, such as their suppliers, who rely on their sources, etc.), whether online or in person. Knowing what you want (and that you're actually getting what you want), why you want it, and that no harmful practices are involved in getting it to you means that the crystal, in your hands, is immensely powerful.

A few points to consider:

- ⟊ There is no global regulation or international certification surrounding fair trade practice of crystals. *Research is key.*

- ⟊ Country of origin is not the same as the name of the mine from which the crystal came, or the factory in which it was cut and polished or otherwise finished.

- ⟊ Some countries you may assume to have lax practices can often have the most environmentally friendly ones.

- ⟊ You get what you pay for. Inexpensive may be good for your wallet immediately, but does the low price reflect shoddy pay or poor or unsafe working conditions for those who mined your crystal, or other unethical practices, such as using child labor or shortcuts to market that harm the planet? Is the stone's authenticity or sustainability compromised? Do compare prices, but try to avoid those that are unusually low for what you're seeking.

- ⟊ DIY: There are places where you are legally allowed to search for buried treasure and unearth your own crystals— nearly every state in the United States has at least one site. It's called rockhounding.

- ⟊ Talk to your sources and ask tough questions. Listen carefully to the answers.

- ⟊ The principle of "do no harm" should extend to the tools you use to cast spells and perform rituals.

BIRTHSTONE ENERGIES

Incorporating your birthstone into your crystal magic work increases those good vibrational energies even more, which you may be able to sense more strongly. Wearing your birthstone is said to bring good luck and good health. The list that follows is based on the traditional stones associated with each birth month and some suggestions for how their individual energies may support your crystal magic.

JANUARY

Garnet

Believed to keep its wearer safe while traveling, garnet has a powerfully energizing and revitalizing energy; it also purifies and invites love and devotion.

FEBRUARY

Amethyst

At one time only available to royalty, this stone is thought to build relationships. Amethyst has a strong healing and calming vibration, boosts inner strength, and offers spiritual protection.

MARCH

Aquamarine

Drinking the water in which aquamarine has been soaked was
believed to cure heart, liver, and stomach ailments. Its energies
help release anger, relieve stress, and raise the tides of courage
to flow with whatever life throws at you.

APRIL

Diamond

A symbol of everlasting love, the diamond is also
believed to instill courage. However, a diamond worn
for effect or prestige will bring the opposite in love.

MAY

Emerald

A sign of wisdom, growth, and patience, the emerald helps release negative energy and opens your heart to love and the power of inner strength.

JUNE

Pearl

The pearl is a traditional symbol of purity and inner wisdom. While not a true crystal, pearls can be worn to magnify loyalty, truth, and sincerity.

JULY

Ruby

Ruby's glorious red color symbolizes love and passion
and promotes energy, sensuality, and vitality.

AUGUST

Peridot

A symbol of strength, peridot ushers in prosperity
and peace.

SEPTEMBER

Sapphire

Another symbol of purity and wisdom, sapphire has a
calming energy. Work with it to strengthen belief in
yourself and foster self-esteem.

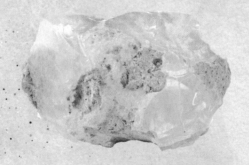

OCTOBER

Opal

The opal represents faithfulness and confidence. This
stone encourages creativity and emits a protective aura.

NOVEMBER

Topaz

Symbolizing love and affection, topaz promotes
honesty, inner wisdom, and openness.

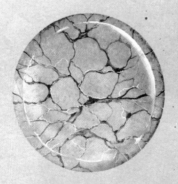

DECEMBER

Turquoise

Turquoise brings luck and good fortune. This healing stone
heightens your spiritual attunement and promotes clear
communication, and so can also promote forgiveness.

CRYSTALS, GEMS, AND STONES

The beauty you are about to behold is just the beginning. With a seemingly unending array of crystals from which to choose, the following stones are but a sampling—one intended to pique your interest, expand your knowledge, offer ideas for how to integrate them into your magical existence, and spur further investigation. Though it's said that beauty is in the eye of the beholder, there is no denying the extensive beauty that exists in the crystal world—evidence of a higher order and magical presence in our Universe, to be sure. And, beyond the surface beauty, lies the beauty of the mystical, magical energies crystals can lend to your practice and your life. Blessed be the bounty we are given. Use it wisely and give thanks for it freely.

So that you may decide how each crystal fits best in your magical tool box, each profile includes:

- Crystal name

- Crystal affirmation to set the stage

- Crystal description, including a bit of history or lore and a note of which zodiac signs may resonate most strongly with the stone

- Crystal magical force

- Crystal chakra correspondence

AGATE

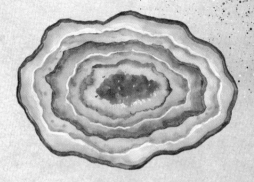

If I dream it, I can live it. I have the courage to try.

Agate, a variety of chalcedony, is a form of quartz and can be found in hundreds of types. The colorful patterns displayed by agate—from bands to dendrites to lace to moss to plumes to pops of fiery iridescence—are intriguing to behold and beautiful to look at. Agate's energy is slower in vibrational frequency than others and is very stabilizing and grounding. It is a terrific choice to use in the home for keeping things calm and steady and producing an environment where self-confidence, acceptance, and achievement rule. It can serve as birthstone to those born in September or under the sign of Gemini.

Magical force: Agate is thought to promote sleep and pleasant dreams, as well as protect against danger and provide courage to face the unknown. If it's the truth you seek, agate can help find it and give you the courage to face it.

Chakra correspondence: Because agate is born of the Earth in all the colors she produces, it can be used to balance all chakras, based on its color. In general, it will clear the aura of negativity and let peace, harmony, and emotional balance flow in to take its place.

AMAZONITE

*I move in harmony with the Universe as I seek to manifest
a life of grace and joy.*

This bluish-green to greenish-blue stone is a variety of
microcline and a member of the feldspar mineral family and is,
indeed, named after the river of the same name—Amazon—the
source of other types of blue-green stones (that aren't amazonite).
Ancient Egyptians valued its color as a symbol of spring, fertility,
and new growth, so frequently used it in jewelry and to make
carvings. Those born under the sign of Virgo can embrace the
stress-free vibes of this lovely crystal as their birthstone.

Magical force: Amazonite is a stone of protection, blocking
and cleansing away general aura pollution. And, like the flowing
waters this stone is named for, amazonite teaches you to go
with the flow. It eases the stress of trying to control things and,
instead, floats your worries downstream, instilling you with the
hope and quiet confidence to keep at it even when plans go awry.

Chakra correspondence: *Heart*—clears away all negativity, so
hope flows in abundance, allowing you to make the best of any
situation, knowing the outcomes will, eventually, be positive. It
can heal the heart of trauma and instill hope, unlocking boundless
loving potential. *Throat*—to speak your truth.

AMBER

I am an old soul, uplifted by all those who came before me.

Amber is formed of resin from ancient pines that has undergone a complex chemical metamorphosis. It is considered an organic gem, but it is not a crystal or stone. Among the oldest of "crystal" treasures, amber specimens are often more than thirty million years old.

It is a stone of healing, as resin's natural purpose is to heal the tree of any wounds sustained. A window into the past, amber often contains fully preserved specimens, both flora and fauna. It is said to be full of life force energies. Tap into it, if you dare. That one-of-a-kind November child can choose this unique gem as an alternative birthstone.

Magical force: Wear or carry amber to help when recovering from injury or illness and to instill in you the forces of longevity carried through its millennia of formation. Amber warms to the touch and can be helpful in keeping you grounded and in the moment. Amber breeds patience, especially important when practicing magic and manifesting dreams, and instills happiness.

Chakra correspondence: *Sacral*—ensures the mind and body are functioning as one; *solar plexus*—keeps your immunity at full capacity to fight off potential illness and releases you from fear of judgment, able to live life on your terms.

AMETHYST

I am soothed by your charms and at peace with my world.

This royal purple stone of the quartz variety has historically been revered for its charms and was, at one time, only available to royalty. Its purple color represents purity, and it is a stone thought to build relationships and protect travelers. Ancient Greeks associated amethyst with Dionysus, god of wine, due to its wine-like color, and believed amethyst's power could even protect against intoxication, so—they thought—one could drink all night, unencumbered, if you drank from a cup carved of amethyst. It is also the stone of St. Valentine and faithful love.

Magical force: This soothing crystal is able to heal and calm emotions and release stress, and brings on sweet dreams. Amulets carved of amethyst are believed to protect people and property from harm. Amethyst boosts inner strength, intuition, and a free flow of emotions, and offers spiritual protection. Amethyst can also help you strengthen relationships and tap in to your inner wisdom. The signs of Aquarius and Pisces are particularly attuned to amethyst's magical energies.

Chakra correspondence: *Third eye*—promotes calming, peaceful energy; particularly helpful with meditation work when honing intentions.

ANGEL AURA CRYSTAL

Though I dream of the future, I embrace today with joy and gratitude.

This clear quartz crystal is chemically bonded with platinum and silver fumes, which give it its rainbow-colored hue and enhanced energies. It is a protective crystal and a natural healer with a soothing vibration. Used in meditation, it is thought to connect you with your spirit guide, and its colors, like those of fairy wings, can transport you to angelic realms. Angel aura quartz can promote loving communication with all in your life. This luminous stone breathes intelligence, creativity, and cohesion. Those born under the sign of Cancer may claim this as their birthstone and appreciate its influence on their naturally social nature.

Magical force: Angel aura is particularly useful for scrying (see page 44) as it has powerful energies for divination. Your questions may also be answered simply by holding the crystal: pose the question—a bright aura indicates "yes"; a dull aura indicates "no."

Chakra correspondence: Due to its multicolored hues, this stone is cleansing and revitalizing for all chakras. *Crown*—connects us to the cosmic realm; *third eye*—enhances the ability to see what we normally take for granted.

AQUAMARINE

I feel safe and empowered to speak my truth; I know I can handle whatever may come.

This beautiful gemstone, the color of the sea, is a variety of the mineral beryl and is aptly named, because *aquamarine* derives from the Latin for "water of the sea." Aquamarine fosters hope, peace, and forgiveness. This stone is touted as the treasure of mermaids and is said to protect sailors and fishers and offer protection in battle. Aquamarine is also believed to enhance a wearer's intellect and personality. Aries, Gemini, and Pisces babies feel the watery influence of aquamarine most closely.

Magical force: Aquamarine is about serenity. The depths of the seas reflected in this stone can help you uncover the depths in your heart. Use aquamarine when facing changes that cause fear and for drawing peace and forgiveness into your life. Combine it with the power of the Waxing Moon to enhance its energies.

Chakra correspondence: *Heart*—helps you recognize your truth; *throat*—promotes clear, honest, heartfelt communication of one's truth; *all*—enhances one's aura.

BLACK ONYX

I embrace the darkness, for that is when I see the light.

An ancient stone, onyx is a type of chalcedony, and its use dates back to some of the earliest civilizations. It did experience a bit of a reputation as a bad luck stone, but that was often just in the eye of the beholder. Black onyx is a powerfully protective stone, giving its owner confidence, strength, and stamina. Because black, as a color, absorbs all the light, it's thought that this quality means black onyx has absorbed all the secrets of Earth from which it is born. Its power, though, can also be one of letting go. Capricorns and Leos may claim black onyx as their birthstone.

Magical force: Onyx fosters self-confidence and self-control, and affords protection while taking action. Onyx will absorb your intentions and remind you of the goals you're working to manifest; it helps ideas take root. Placed in a crystal grid (see page 72), it emanates protection while absorbing negative energy. It is magnificent for scrying (see page 44). Do not fear the dark: when working with black onyx, you'll feel the wonder of the night sky and its infinite possibilities.

Chakra correspondence: *Root*—grounds you in self-confidence and wise decision making and the energy to move forward.

BLACK TOURMALINE

I am safe, protected, and free to act as me.

Black tourmaline is of the boron silicate family. Black (also called schorl) is the most commonly occurring color of tourmaline, though it is widely available in a rainbow of colors (see Tourmaline, page 137). Historically, those practicing the magical arts used black tourmaline to keep evil away. It is one of the most powerfully protecting stones, forming a shield of sorts, blocking negative and harmful energies, and reflecting them back to their source—where they belong! Tourmaline can be a distinct asset in times of struggle, not only suggesting solutions but also pinpointing the real cause of the distress. October babies may wish to wear this unique stone as a birthstone.

Magical force: Because of black tourmaline's protective powers, you will feel safe, secure, and emboldened to take risks with the energy and clarity to tackle what's needed to manifest your goals. Black tourmaline is also a cleansing stone and can help clear negative thoughts, boost self-esteem, and lessen anxiety, while facilitating a positive outlook. It is a strongly grounding stone and can be particularly useful in meditation. Cast a circle with black tourmaline for ritual work.

Chakra correspondence: *Root*—establishes feelings of safety and security due to its grounding properties.

BLOODSTONE

I am a courageous warrior able to withstand the battles of life.

A magical stone filled with ancient lore, bloodstone is also known as heliotrope, as it was believed to turn the Sun red when placed in water. It is a form of chalcedony and most desirably dark green in color with flecks of red from iron oxide, resembling drops of blood, hence the name. The first bloodstone is believed to have formed when, while Jesus was on the Cross, drops of His blood dripped onto the stone, staining it. Revered as a healing stone, bloodstone was carried into battle as it was thought to stop bleeding when injured. Bloodstone pulsates with vitality and energy. In India, it is valued for its aphrodisiac qualities. It is an alternative birthstone for those born in March.

Magical force: To become fully centered and grounded for meditation, start with bloodstone in your hand. When ready, swap bloodstone for a crystal fully aligned with your intentions. Incorporated into your spellwork, bloodstone is especially powerful for weather magic, matters of family love, money, calming fears, and instilling courage—no matter the battle being fought.

Chakra correspondence: *Root*—aligns energies so basic needs are met, leaving you feeling safe, secure, grounded, and belonging.

BLUE KYANITE

I am receptive to the messages of the Universe that guide me to my highest self.

Blue kyanite forms from the mineral aluminum silicate. This high-vibrational stone inspires loyalty and thus promotes the ability and desire to heal relationship rifts, whether personal, professional, familial, or other. Blue kyanite also anchors you in the reality of fulfilling your destiny, so quit blaming it on others and get to work! The color of the sky, blue kyanite allows you to soar, and gives you the patience needed to get to your desired destination. If Pisces is your sign, blue kyanite is considered a birthstone option—its watery hue is a kindred spirit.

Magical force: Use kyanite's vibrational ability in meditation to enhance your clair (psychic) gifts and connect with your spirit wisdom. Its powerful energies are strongly protective—like a shield of armor against life's slings and arrows. Blue kyanite fills you with water's flowing spirit and ability to move around obstacles with ease. Place this crystal under your pillow if you're working to recall and interpret dreams or wish to experience lucid dreams.

Chakra correspondence: Uniquely, *all*, and especially the *throat chakra*. Kyanite increases the truth and clarity of your communication, especially among opposing viewpoints.

CARNELIAN

I act with the passion of purpose.

Carnelian is a form of chalcedony whose name derives from the Latin *cornum*, referencing the cornel cherry it resembles. It is an old stone with a rich history. Egyptians sought its protective aura to guide the dead on their journey forward, and the Romans favored this stone for signet rings used to seal official documents—hot wax will not stick to it. It also has a reputation for being one of the luckiest gems available and carries an association with royalty. Carnelian is the warm orange-red color of glowing embers and it will ignite your powers of creativity. It creates a sense of cozy happiness, like gathering around the hearth with friends and family. Cancer, Leo, Taurus, and Virgo may all be charmed by this stone as an alternative birthstone.

Magical force: Carnelian increases personal power and self-confidence, while grounding you in the present moment to be fully in charge. True to its fiery red color, carnelian can also release your passionate side, for whatever excites you, and act as that kick in the pants you need to get things done. Carnelian can also promote fertility for whatever you desire to give birth to.

Chakra correspondence: *Sacral*—governs creativity and wisdom.

CELESTITE

If I can dream it, I can live it.

From the Latin word *caelestis*, meaning "celestial," celestite is a conduit of heavenly communication and a vibrant connection to our intuitive senses. Celestite's makeup is of strontium sulfate and it is the primary natural source of strontium, an element used to create red (not blue, that's copper) fireworks. Its soothing energies are a balm for our worries and can aid in healing sadness and grief. Its dreamy qualities are especially conducive to peaceful sleep. Those born under the signs of Libra and Gemini can benefit from its emotion-stabilizing influence.

Magical force: Use it in meditation to seek tranquility, divine guidance, universal blessings, or messages from loved ones who have passed. Place celestite in children's rooms to ease fears, or in your bedroom where, if you listen closely, you'll hear its lullaby from the angels. Just holding celestite, in a quiet space, can enhance your sense of mindfulness.

Chakra correspondence: *Throat*—boosts our ability to express what we feel. *Third eye*—allows higher energies to flow in, promoting ease and giving us the wisdom to accept what we cannot change or control and the vision to change what we can. *Crown*—helps access the realm beyond.

CHRYSOCOLLA

I am a sum of all my emotions, without judgment.

Chrysocolla is a silicate mineral and forms in places where water dissolves copper from Earth, which contributes to its blue-greenish hue. This gentle, healing stone can bring on peaceful, easy feelings just by looking at it. Chrysocolla's cool color can help you keep your cool and, as such, is a good stone for daily use. As a stone said to encourage staying close to home, it stirs a great acceptance of self. Taurus, Gemini, and Virgo birth signs may choose chrysocolla as an alternative birthstone to remind them of their softer side.

Magical force: Chrysocolla can help dispel fear, anger, worry, pain, and bad habits—including bad relationships—and empower you to accept the changes needed or just say no to those who don't respect your boundaries, and fill the space by drawing in ease, comfort, wisdom, and forgiveness. It is a stone of new beginnings and the joy they can bring. It can also be used in love spells. Placed in any room of the home, it creates an instant energy oasis.

Chakra correspondence: Said to align all the chakras with the divine, chrysocolla is particularly healing for removing energy blocks of the *third eye*, *throat*, and *heart* chakras.

CITRINE

I greet the Sun with gratitude for another magical day.

Citrine, of the quartz family, radiates sunny optimism. This yellow-hued stone is warming, nurturing, and energizing. It uplifts and bursts with life. Citrine can help clarify your thoughts, especially when seeking new paths. It is a restful stone and good to keep nearby when concentration is required or the creative juices are flowing. Natural citrine is rare and well worth the search, but abundantly available as a heat-treated variety of amethyst or smoky quartz. It instills optimism and attracts prosperity, earning it the nickname "merchant's stone." If November is your birth month, absorb the sunny rays of citrine's good fortune.

Magical force: Citrine manifests abundance and, in turn, increases generosity—sharing wealth brings wealth. Its optimistic nature instills joy and self-confidence that what you desire can be yours.

Chakra correspondence: *Solar plexus*—clears the way for health-promoting energies to flow freely throughout your body.

CLEAR QUARTZ

It is clear: I am beautiful. I am wise. I am love. I am light. I am enough.

Clear quartz crystal, silicon dioxide, is among the most abundantly available of magical crystals given to us by Earth, and yet the most spectacularly endowed. Though seemingly mundane, step closer and you'll see the wisdom of the ages written on its soul. It is most typically found as a six-sided prism, pointed at both ends, an example of sacred geometry at its best and a source of its exquisite power.

It is believed to be a universal soother and healer and, among other things, encourages positive thoughts, enhances energy, nurtures patience, and brings clear vision into focus. In a nod to its all-purpose nature, this crystal can be helpful to all signs of the zodiac to amplify intentions, counteract negative energy, and find acceptance.

Magical force: Clear quartz is among the most powerful crystals when working to manifest intentions. Clear quartz can boost the energy of other stones around it and can stand in for any stone's magical message when that stone is unavailable. Clear quartz is the epitome of a scrying crystal and awaits your gaze upon it.

Chakra correspondence: Because of its ability to split light into the color spectrum, it will work to align all the chakras.

CORDIERITE (IOLITE)

I chart my own course.

Cordierite is a silicate mineral. In its gem quality, this blue-violet stone is known as iolite—from *ios*, Greek for "violet." Known, too, as the Viking compass stone, it was purportedly used by ancient Viking seafarers as a type of filter with which to locate the Sun on cloudy days, enabling them to determine their position at sea and adjust course, as needed. It can help you navigate a number of life's challenges, as well, such as banishing bad habits, managing money for abundance, restoring motivation, and sorting out priorities—and it guides travelers safely home from any journey. Iolite gives you the courage to explore and the vision to see your dreams into reality. Sagittarius, Taurus, and Libra may choose this stone as their guide.

Magical force: Use this dusk-colored stone at twilight when casting spells for banishment to double its effect. Use iolite to establish a wealth mentality and expand your thinking as to what you can accomplish. Iolite can be effective at healing family drama, acting as the compass to guide everyone home. Use iolite in meditation to journey deep into yourself and discover your True North.

Chakra correspondence: *Third eye*—helps us find our place in a world that's bigger than we are.

DIAMOND

I emerge from the fire stronger than before. I will survive and shine brighter than ever.

Diamond forms from carbon under intense pressure about 100 miles (161 km) under Earth's surface. Imagine if we all emerged so lovely under such circumstances! It is the hardest substance on Earth and a symbol of everlasting love—the name comes from the Greek *adamas*, or unbreakable. Since their discovery circa 2500 BCE in India, where diamonds washed up on river shores with ordinary gravel, they have been cherished for their fiery brilliance, and their mystique has ruled through the ages.

Diamond is believed to instill courage. However, a diamond worn for effect or prestige will bring the opposite in love. Diamond is the traditional birthstone of April babies—lucky, indeed.

Magical force: A natural amplifier of physical and spiritual energies, the diamond's higher vibrational frequencies can heal relationships, offer protective properties, and instill great courage. It boosts the power of other stones and can be a great asset to your crystal grid work (see page 72). Diamond is a stone of light: let it guide you.

Chakra correspondence: *Crown*—opens us to the messages of the Universe.

FAIRY STONE

I believe in magic.

Fairy stones, in the shape of a naturally formed cross (Maltese, Roman, and St. Andrew's are the most common), are formed from the mineral staurolite (*stauros* means "cross" in Greek). The stones can be found across the Southeastern United States and in Switzerland, Russia, Mexico, and Brazil, among other countries. Their true origins are said to be the fairies' tears on learning of the death of Christ, which crystallized into crosses as they hit the ground. If you like to connect with the fae or other spirit guides in your work, fairy stones create a magical flow of protective energy, inviting them into your space.

Magical force: Fairy stones can connect your mind and heart to the spirit realm. They also bring good luck and offer protection from illness and negative energies—and evil spirits—as well as call wealth and abundance to you. Giving fairy stones as gifts strengthens your bond with the receiver and is like passing on a bit of luck. Staurolite has a strong connection to magical rituals, believed to increase their power.

Chakra correspondence: *Heart*—opens it to love and care for Earth and all her inhabitants, both flora and fauna; *root*—grounds and calms you; *third eye*—focuses your connection with those beyond our realm.

─ GARNET ─

I step bravely into discomfort, for that is where I grow.

Garnet is among a group of rock-forming minerals, often found in metamorphic rock, and is one of the oldest known gemstones. Though found in a variety of colors, red is the color most typically associated with this crystal. Rumored to be the source of a dragon's fiery eyes, this ancient talisman is said to bring luck and has been worn for centuries as a protective and curative talisman. Its burning color, the color of blood and life force, is an outward symbol of this stone's association with love and passion. Garnet is also believed to keep its wearer safe while traveling. Garnet serves as January's traditional birthstone.

Magical force: Powerfully energizing and revitalizing, garnet also purifies and balances and invites love and devotion. It can foster the courage to pursue whatever your passion is and the commitment to make it reality. If travel is your passion, carry garnet along for a safe ride. Placed under a pillow, garnet is said to ease disturbing dreams. Wear garnet to attract a lover. Garnet's lucky properties are especially conducive to business ventures and promise prosperity.

Chakra correspondence: All, especially the *root* and *heart* chakras. Garnet calms or ignites the flow of energy as needed.

GREEN AVENTURINE

*I face each day with gratitude for the abundance bestowed upon me;
my luck and my worth are immense.*

Although aventurine comes in many colors, if green aventurine
is in your crystal collection, count yourself lucky, as this stone
is one of the luckiest of all. This lovely crystal is a type of quartz
that connects you to the soothing energy of Nature. Called the
"gambler's stone," this ancient crystal is said to bring luck in all
manner and form and can even make sure you're in the right
place at the right time to take advantage of said luck! It glows
of optimism and good fortune and keeps you perpetually on the
sunny side of the street. Pick up green aventurine whenever a
little lucky magic wouldn't hurt your chances of success, or when
you need to ditch a bad habit that may be standing between you
and your dreams.

   Magical force: Green aventurine is particularly useful in money
spells, or carried as a lucky charm at the casino! It can also
strengthen your courage to seize the lucky moments when they
come and boost overall feelings of happiness and satisfaction.

   Chakra correspondence: *Heart*—boosts late-in-life romance
and calms family strife. And, with an open heart, you'll hear Lady
Luck most clearly when she calls your name.

GREEN JADE

I am richly blessed and share freely with others.

Jade is a type of metamorphic rock that comes in a rainbow of colors—green is the most highly valued. In addition to jewelry made from jade, its durability also made it significant for fashioning into weapons and exquisitely melodic musical instruments. Jade can variously symbolize heaven, nobility, longevity, virtue, wealth, and protection and is called the stone of the heart. Legend tells us that jade that becomes chipped has just taken the brunt of a blow meant for you. As an alternative birthstone, it's said that Virgos, as well as those born between the hours of 9 p.m. and 10 p.m., should wear jade.

Magical force: The color green typically symbolizes lush growth and vitality, and green jade brings all that in all areas of life. It is thought to protect and speak wisely to the loving heart, with lessons that sharing our abundance is at the root of true happiness. Gentle jade is a calm, serene stone, so keep some nearby if your nerves or confidence are a-jangle. It is as useful in meditation work as it is in dreamwork. Count yourself lucky to have jade in your possession: its magic will amplify yours.

Chakra correspondence: *Heart*—maintains healing and balance.

HEMATITE

I am grounded and focused and live mindfully each day.

Hematite is an iron oxide, usually formed in the presence of water, and among the most abundant minerals on Earth. Although steely gray to black, and sometimes red, in color, it produces reddish streaks when tested and in its abundance on Mars is credited for the planet's nickname: the red planet. Appropriately, hematite derives from *haimatitis*, Greek for "blood red," which is hematite's color when ground into a powder. It is a deeply grounding stone that provides ease and confidence. Aries and Aquarius may wear hematite as an alternative birthstone.

Magical force: Hematite is the stone of the mind and encourages learning, focus, and deep thought; it releases practical wisdom and boosts self-confidence. Let hematite protect you, as well, from harmful energies meant to attack: placed in the corners of your home, or a specific room, hematite emits a protective shield while absorbing the harmful energy. Hematite can be useful in both scrying (see page 44) and meditation work (see page 54) by clearing away the cobwebs and revealing the truth that needs to be seen.

Chakra correspondence: *Root*—grounds energy flow deeply connected to Earth.

LABRADORITE

I welcome transformation and the opportunities it brings.

Labradorite is a variety of feldspar named for its place of discovery in Labrador, Canada. This mystical, magical, multihued stone is as flashy as a peacock in full display (the colorful effect is called labradorescence) and believed, by the Inuit, to have fallen to Earth from the aurora borealis. As such, it brings powers to increase clairvoyance, and its energies will surround you in a magical cloak of protection, blocking negative energy. But labradorite will also keep you grounded, so as not to lose your head in the clouds. This beauty is the stone of new beginnings and limitless potential. Labradorite discourages antisocial behavior and encourages courtesy and friendliness. Pisces, Leo, Scorpio, and Taurus are among the lucky that can wear labradorite as a birthstone.

Magical force: Gazing into this mystical stone is like peeking through the curtain to the other side. Try scrying or meditating with labradorite. It is a marker of change and a reminder of strength to embrace it. Place a piece under your pillow to tap into the unconscious realm of your dreams.

Chakra correspondence: All, but especially the *third eye*. Labradorite aligns mental, physical, and spiritual power for the highest vibrational energies.

LAPIS LAZULI

I trust my instincts and inner wisdom.

Lapis Lazuli, a stone of communication, intuition, and personal power, is a metamorphic rock that is composed of numerous minerals, including lazurite, pyrite, and calcite. Its distinct deep-blue color, sometimes with flecks of pyrite, make it a sought-after gemstone, and it's been popular as such for thousands of years. Libra and Sagittarius may choose lapis lazuli as their birthstone.

Note: Because one of the primary—and oldest—sources for the finest lapis is Afghanistan, where it is often mined and obtained illegally, there are advocacy groups working to have Afghan lapis labeled as a conflict mineral (see page 189 for more on this topic).

Magical force: Lapis lazuli has a very calming energy, easing all manner of mental and emotional distress and facilitating communication in difficult circumstances. Meditating with lapis can lift your spirit to the heavens and connect you to your spirit guides to receive enlightening messages. It is a stone of friendship and can attract like-minded people to you. Lapis will reinforce your personal power to act for your highest good and draw the respect of others to you.

Chakra correspondence: *Throat*—enhances truth and wisdom in all forms of communication, including with yourself; *third eye*—works as a conduit to one's higher self.

LEMURIAN SEED CRYSTAL

I am one with the Universe.

The origins of Lemurian Seed Crystal are steeped in mystic lore, in the peaceful and mythical kingdom of Lemuria, located in the South Pacific region. Legend tells us that the Lemurians foresaw a disastrous event and, in order to preserve their knowledge, wisdom, and traditions, embedded, or coded, them all into these crystals.

These wand-like crystals come in a variety of colors and can be identified by their tactile parallel striations, or markings, noted as resembling bar codes. Some say their source is a single mine in Brazil; others say these crystals can be found the world over. Whatever your beliefs, the energy these crystals emit is unmistakable and magical in its own right. All signs of the zodiac may claim Lemurian seed crystal as their birthstone.

Magical force: Lemurian seed crystal is a conduit to your spirit guide and the wisdom of the Universe, if you're wise enough to listen. It is also a healing crystal. While meditating with Lemurian seed crystal, gently guide your thumb up along the crystal's striations to reveal their ancient wisdom. Use in all spellwork seeking peace, harmony, joy, oneness, friendship, and acceptance.

Chakra correspondence: All, and particularly the *third eye*. At its best, Lemurian seed crystal harmonizes and heals.

MALACHITE

There are no limits to manifesting my dreams.

Malachite is a copper carbonate hydroxide mineral, first thought to be mined about four thousand years ago in Egypt and what is now Israel. This mesmerizing beauty stands out in a crowd, yet malachite's swirling visual energy is soothing and comforting all at once. It has served as a protective talisman to many throughout history. If you're a Capricorn or Scorpio, let malachite inspire your path when worn as a birthstone.

Note: If working with malachite, handle it only in its polished, finished form.

Magical force: Working with malachite allows our subconscious to reveal what we need and grasp what our emotions are trying to tell us. It instills leadership and the confidence to take action for change. It draws away negative energy, so it needs to be cleansed more often than some other stones. Try scrying with malachite (see page 44). It is a stone of dreamers, as it allows your creativity and psychic intuition to soar.

Chakra correspondence: All, especially the *heart*. Malachite clears the pathways to give and receive love and fosters true loyalty and generosity; *throat*—encourages truth and honesty in all you do.

MOLDAVITE

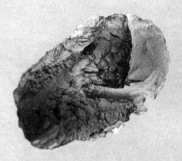

*I emerge from the fire, reborn of the stars. I accept healing
energy into my life.*

A true star is born! Moldavite, among the rarest of materials on
Earth, is used as a gem, but is, technically, a glass. This high-
vibrational crystal is a fusion of heaven and Earth, as it was
born of an explosive meteorite collision with Earth about fifteen
million years ago. The Czech Republic, near the Moldau River, is
the single source of this transformative stone. Its energies are
said to bring healing, particularly connecting the mind and heart.
Moldavite can effect swift change, and boost energy. Its forest-
green color speaks of growth and renewal. As it is born of the
stars, every sign of the zodiac may benefit from its use.

   Magical force: This high-vibrational stone can help raise not
only your energy but also the energy of other stones around it.
Let it connect you to your spirit guides or guardian angels and
interpret their messages. In meditation, moldavite provides a
layer of spiritual protection and can produce powerful visions
and insights.

   Chakra correspondence: *Heart*, especially one in need of
healing; *third eye*—opens channels of cosmic communication and
other-dimensional energies as well as your mind to new ideas
and the flow of creative energy.

MOONSTONE

I am a magical being of divine origins able to manifest my dreams.

Mysterious, glowing moonstone is a variety of the feldspar mineral group. It is found in a number of colors, including gray, peach, rainbow, and white. Moonstone, once believed to have originated from moonbeams themselves, is a stone of new beginnings, fertility, destiny, and wishes. It is also one of reflection, helping you look within and find forgiveness. Enchantingly beautiful, moonstone traditionally helps us connect to the natural ebb and flow of the Moon's energy. If you're dealing with high emotions, or are in need of restoring calm and balance, this could be the stone for you. It is often associated with zodiac water signs and serves as the birthstone for those born in the month of June.

Magical force: Place moonstone under your pillow to inspire prophetic dreams. Incorporate moonstone into any Moon magic work, and to summon your inner goddess. Carry moonstone for good luck. Legend says if you hold a moonstone in your mouth on the night of the Full Moon, your future will be revealed.

Chakra correspondence: *Third eye*—restores a balance of emotions and instills patience; *crown*—increases intuitive abilities, expands your vision, and allows you to feel at peace with your place in the Universe.

OPAL

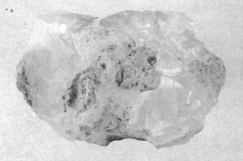

My fire burns bright. I will let it shine.

The opal is born of water, specifically the silica deposits it leaves in its wake. Its magnificent display of colors comes from submicroscopic spheres arranged in patterns within the stone and the way light refracts within them. Opal has been recognized by many cultures and throughout time for its superior charms. Today, the opal represents faithfulness and confidence, creativity and self-expression. It is October's birthstone, and many believe it's bad luck to wear opal unless born under its sign. That association with bad luck, however, may have originated in France, where wearers believed the stone, wrapped in a bay leaf, rendered them invisible, allowing them to steal without being caught.

Magical force: Place opal over your closed eyes to ease eyestrain. Use it in meditation with any Earth goddess to connect to her natural soothing energies. If you have one, use it for good.

Chakra correspondence: All, depending on its color play, or specific to each chakra, depending on its dominant color, such as black for the *root* chakra, fire opal for the *sacral* chakra, yellow for the *solar plexus* chakra, green or pink for the *heart* chakra, blue for the *throat* chakra, violet for the *third eye* chakra, and white for the *crown* chakra.

PEACOCK ORE

I choose to see beyond that which is physical;
I believe in the power of magic.

A copper iron sulfide mineral, peacock ore is born among
sedimentary, metamorphic, and igneous rock environments.
Peacock ore is named such for its beautiful iridescent coloring
when tarnished. Its stunning coloring speaks to our inner child
and elicits joyful emotions and the innocence of living in the
moment. Peacock ore can be very balancing and healing, as it's
said that when placed on or near one chakra, it will balance and
align all the chakras. Also called the witches' stone, peacock ore
can help you connect to your ancient wisdom and most magical
self. It can serve as the birthstone to those born under the sign of
Cancer, supporting this sign's natural nurturing tendences.

   Magical force: Peacock ore allows us to channel our inner
energies toward manifesting goals. It is a stone of happiness
and will help you see the positive in any negative situations. It is
also a stone of new beginnings and rebirth and can be especially
powerful when combined with New Moon magic rituals.

   Chakra correspondence: *Root*—starts the pathway to clearing
energy blocks from all the chakras and brings our emotions into
balance; *third eye*—enhances insight and intuition.

PERIDOT

Strength and abundance radiate from me with ease.

Peridot, a form of olivine, is literally pushed up from deep within the Earth's mantle, as it splits, moves, and morphs, often via volcanic means, bearing this beautiful greenish-yellow stone. It symbolizes strength. One of the oldest gemstones on record, peridot was called the "gem of the Sun" by ancient Egyptians, having believed it was thrown to Earth when the Sun exploded, carrying all its healing qualities. This stone, one of only a few that is found in just one color, serves as birthstone for those born in August.

Magical force: When you just feel out of step with all that is going on around you, peridot can help re-sync you to the natural rhythms of life—and its powers are said to wax and wane along with the Moon's cycle. It can usher in prosperity in all its forms. As a stone of transformation, peridot can help you break those bad habits that may be holding you back from manifesting your true potential. Peridot can help you connect to the fairy realm.

Chakra correspondence: *Heart*—opens it to receive fully what is given and release all that no longer serves, such as anger, jealousy, hurt, and ego.

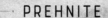

I am healed.

Prehnite is a silicate mineral, typically beautifully green in color, discovered in South Africa in the eighteenth century. Called the stone of prophecy, it has a lovely magical energy and can induce that sense of déjà vu. Prehnite is particularly useful when manifesting intentions that come from the heart. Prehnite's energies will help align yours with Nature, as well as opening your heart to unconditional love and your mind to new ideas. Libras may wish to wear prehnite as a birthstone.

Magical force: Prehnite provides special energy to attract angels and fairies (and offers an orb of protective energy from random encounters with evil fairies). It is said to enhance your prophetic senses, such as clairvoyance, clairaudience, and claircognizance, so add it to your scrying crystals or tarot sessions for clearer communications with spirit guides (pay special attention to your dreams afterward). Used in meditation, prehnite keeps you grounded in the present and abundantly happy. Prehnite is particularly powerful in crystal grids for abundance (see page 72).

Chakra correspondence: *Heart*—heals wounds of past loves lost, opens you to receive new love, eases anxiety.

PYRITE

I am a money magnet.

Pyrite, a sulfide mineral with a brassy color and metallic luster, is also known as fool's gold. However, it is a treasure trove of abundant energy for your life and is particularly valuable in manifesting wealth. Its ability to create sparks when struck against other stones or metal can literally spark change, ideas, and inspiration.

Pyrite provides a mirror into your soul to see the truths that reside there, including things you may be looking away from. It is also called the healer's stone. Those born under the sign of Leo can wear pyrite as a birthstone with pride.

Magical force: Meditate with pyrite when money is the issue—it will stimulate a wealth of possible solutions. You may also pick up some messages about false friends in your life; heed those warnings as they come, so as not to be "fooled" by an enemy in disguise. In large enough pieces, pyrite is an excellent tool for scrying (see page 44). Wear or carry it to surround yourself with a protective aura.

Chakra correspondence: *Sacral* and *solar plexus*—Pyrite can help untangle the negative energy you have building inside. Whether your stomach is the worse for wear or you need help trusting your gut, choose pyrite's healing energies.

ROSE QUARTZ

I see the world through rose-colored glasses—with positive intent, love, and compassion for all.

If you listen carefully, you may hear the heartbeat of the Universe in this stone of love. This pink-hued stone, a form of quartz, is a nurturing stone offered by Mother Earth as her expression of unconditional love. Rose quartz beads found in Iraq can be dated back as far as 7000 BCE, and were, perhaps, used as talismans. Its energies can help heal emotional trauma, ease anxiety, release jealousy, mend a forsaken heart, and clear away anything negative that prevents the sending or receiving of love. It can serve as the birthstone for those born under the signs of Libra, Scorpio, or Taurus.

Magical force: Rose quartz has a high vibration but a gentle energy that complements meditation, especially if working to soothe angry emotions. Use it in spellwork to attract love or in a ritual bath to add an aura of irresistibility to the love vibes you emanate. As part of a candle magic ritual, it can help send loving energies into the world when it's hurting and needs to be healed.

Chakra correspondence: *Heart*—heals any wounds or pain stored there and opens one up to the healing powers of empathy and compassion, restoring the heart's ability to give and receive love.

SALT

I celebrate life's flavorful abundance.

Though not a valuable gemstone or stone, salt is an invaluable (edible) natural mineral crystal, made mainly of sodium chloride. Its mystical powers are long and storied. Its use in divination is called halomancy: tossed into a fire, you interpret the reactions in the flames; poured onto a plate, you interpret the patterns. Every seasoned witch (and new witches, too) should make a place for salt in their apothecary. If you're born in April, diamond is a traditional birthstone; choose a salt and pepper diamond for a fun swap. Although grains of salt may be small, their magic is mighty.

Magical force: Salt can represent Earth on your altar and its energies are grounding. Make an offering of salt to your favorite goddess or use it to cleanse and purify your crystals and home (see page 31). It can absorb negative energy and call in abundance and prosperity. Himalayan salt is particularly energetic—keep some (a salt lamp is great for this) in rooms that get high traffic from different people to neutralize the negative energies that may be present. When casting a circle, use salt to double the protective barrier you seek to create.

Chakra correspondence: *All*—has purifying, cleansing energy; lets peace and calm flow freely.

SAPPHIRE

I will reach for the heavens until I touch the stars.

This stunning blue crystal, sapphire, is of the corundum family. Traditionally a stone of the nobility, sapphire was worn for protection from poisoning *and* envy as well as to attract great wealth. Sapphire symbolizes faithfulness, truth, and wisdom and is a stone of romance and heavenly blessings. Sapphire is reputed to invite happiness, peace, and prosperity into your world and bestow overall fine health, and specifically good mental health and eyesight. Its energies can help focus the mind, especially when navigating change, and expand your ability to see beauty and interpret your intuition. Sapphire serves as the birthstone for those born in September, as well as those born under the signs of Taurus or Gemini.

Magical force: Sapphire's energy has a calming effect, instilling ease and joy. Work with it to strengthen belief in yourself and foster self-esteem. It can transform negative energy into self-discipline to manifest your desired goals. A sapphire elixir is an excellent purifier for your altar or other sacred places.

Chakra correspondence: *Third eye*—unlocks deeper levels of consciousness and self-discovery; *throat*—helps us make our truths known to the world.

SELENITE

I trust my inner wisdom and will listen to my heart, for it speaks the ancient truth of my guardian spirits.

This stone honors the Greek Moon goddess, Selene, and embodies the Moon goddess qualities of blessings, love, peace, and light. A type of gypsum, this typically colorless, transparent, yet lustrous crystal is highly vibrational and can sometimes feel warm when touched. Selenite is often used when reaching for spiritual guidance or help from a guardian angel. It can also put you in touch with your own inner wisdom. In meditation with selenite, you'll feel protected in its Moon-like glow and attuned to the wisdom of the ages, allowing you to reach for the stars as you manifest your dreams. Taurus is particularly attuned to selenite.

Magical force: This healing and protective crystal is easy to work with and beneficial to all. It helps rebalance the body and connect with higher protective guardians. One simple use is clearing or releasing all negative energy nearby. Selenite is also thought to attract love and friendship and promote honesty and truth, resulting in good relationships. *Keep safe away from water.*

Chakra correspondence: *Crown*—helps us see and appreciate our place in the Universe and connect to a higher, universal, wisdom; unblocks a stagnant crown chakra, which will help balance all the energies throughout the body.

SHUNGITE

I receive the positive energies of those who lift me up; I reject the
negative energies of those who seek to drag me down.

Shungite, a mostly carbon-based stone, was first discovered in
the early 1700s in the Russian village of Shun'ga, thus its name.
It is an effective cleansing and purifying stone and has even been
shown to exhibit antioxidant and anti-inflammatory properties.
Shungite can absorb and disperse negative energy anywhere
near you and help you clarify your thoughts and intentions. When
your aura is cleansed of negativity, it is open to filling with light
and happiness.

Shungite also amplifies the energies of any other crystals
you place it with. No matter your zodiac sign, shungite can be a
powerful addition to your magical tool box.

Magical force: Shungite's intense black color makes it perfect
for protective magical spells. Meditating with shungite can help
ease stress, ridding your body of the negative energy dragging
you down. Adding shungite dust to your garden (fairy or
otherwise) is said to make your plants grow abundantly.

Chakra correspondence: *Root*—has intense grounding
properties, boosts vitality, and clears the path for the opportunity
to connect with a higher spirit, accessing the wisdom of
the Universe.

SMOKY QUARTZ

*Though darkness brings uncertainty, I am protected
and empowered to act.*

Smoky quartz is a transparent, brown-colored variety of quartz, a
silicon dioxide mineral, and gets its name from its smoky-colored
appearance. Known as the stone of power, it is the national gem of
Scotland, making it a significant feature in traditional Highlander
wear, and the state gem of New Hampshire. For ancient Druids,
it was a sacred symbol of the power held by Earth gods and
goddesses. It is often used to honor Hecate, Greek Triple Goddess
of the Moon and the night, the spiritual world, and magic. Any
sign of the zodiac will benefit from smoky quartz's protection
when worn as an alternative birthstone.

Magical force: A strongly grounding, cleansing, and protective
stone, smoky quartz can call in healing, shielding energies to
your spellwork. It is especially protective of the home. Smoky
quartz shares a connection to Samhain due to its dark appearance
and the corresponding beginning of the darker time of year, so it
is particularly powerful for spells worked on that date, October 31.

Chakra correspondence: *Root*—provides deep grounding in the
physical world and a feeling of power and strength.

SODALITE

I speak truth to power, so those who cannot are heard.

Sodalite is a member of the feldspathoid mineral group and is classified as a rare rock-forming mineral. It contains a high amount of sodium, from which its name is derived. The stone's color is a beautiful royal blue–violet and its energy will awaken your clair senses. Often mistaken for lapis lazuli, sodalite has an unmistakable calming, harmonious vibration. Sodalite clears the mental cobwebs, stops that negative internal monologue, and powers up reason, analysis, and observation. It helps you see things as they are, so you can make decisions aligned with your highest good. Sagittarians may choose sodalite as a birthstone, as it speaks to their optimistic nature.

Magical force: Sodalite is ideal for meditation when diving deep into your soul is your purpose. It takes you to your inner truth, revealing both strengths and weaknesses. If you are prone to worry, sodalite can bring you out of yourself, revealing your rational side and instilling a sense of calm control. It may help in communication with your spirit guides and can be used for lucid dreaming.

Chakra correspondence: *Throat*—aligns words and their meaning with intent to unite, not divide, and helps in finding your voice, if needed.

SPIRIT QUARTZ

I extend my hand in friendship to all.

This sparkling beauty is a recently discovered (circa 2000) quartz crystal from South Africa and is like a community of crystals all in one. It comprises a single, large crystal that is covered with a second layer of smaller, glittering mini druzy crystals. There are four forms and colors of spirit quartz: *amethyst spirit quartz* (lavender to deep purple), *citrine spirit quartz* (gold/yellow), *smoky spirit quartz* (gray to brown), and *white spirit quartz*, sometimes called fairy spirit quartz (clear to opaque). Like clear quartz, spirit quartz in all its forms is a highly vibrational stone and powerful healer. It is also a stone of joy that will connect you to higher realms, especially in dreamwork. Pisces may be drawn to amethyst spirit quartz as an alternative birthstone and Cancer babies may turn toward the sunny glow of citrine spirit quartz.

Magical force: Feel yourself fully connected to the Universe as the generosity of your mind and soul opens you to new experiences and the joy being with others can bring. This crystal has strong energies of growth.

Chakra correspondence: White—*all*, as a stone of alignment; citrine—*sacral* and *solar plexus* chakras; amethyst—*crown* chakra; smoky quartz—*root* and *third eye* chakras.

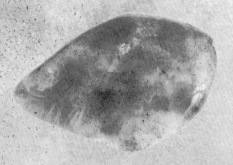

I radiate joy.

Sunstone, also known as heliolite, is a feldspar, usually translucent, that exhibits lovely bright flashes in light like little bursts of sunshine. Sunstone has been known for only a few hundred years; the most famous, and best, deposits are in Oregon, discovered by Indigenous Peoples living in that region, who treasured its beauty as a gift from Mother Earth. This fiery stone breeds passion and life and is a happy-go-lucky crystal. Wear sunstone to increase your vitality and let your inner being shine. Sunday's child may wear sunstone as a nontraditional birthstone to support a joyful life.

Magical force: Sunstone will ignite your passion and power. Its warming vibrations encourage you to open yourself to opportunities and revel in the moment. It is a source of strength and light in times of darkness and can boost your intuition in meditation. Sunstone encourages optimism and enthusiasm and releases you from fear of others' judgment. It envelops you in a reflective barrier, off of which all negative energy ricochets.

Chakra correspondence: *All*, especially the *root* chakra, like the Sun, the source of all energy for the body and seat of personal power.

— TIGER'S EYE —

I choose, each day, to see the light and grace in all.

Lustrous tiger's eye, most typically of golden-brown quartz, is reputed to give the ability to see, observe, and sense. It also provides clarity that can offer another perspective. Its gifts are protection, abundance, and power. Tiger's eye was carried into battle by Roman soldiers and frequently used as a protective talisman against curses and bad luck. Capricorns, with their intense productivity inclination, may find this stone useful, and fearless Leos will recognize the energies as their own.

Magical force: Call on tiger's eye when your personal power reserves feel depleted. It can help relieve fear, anxiety, and self-doubt, whether in matters of love or business. Tiger's eye sees within its realm protection, good luck, and prosperity. It is also a reminder to see the beauty in ourselves as others see us. Tiger's eye can harmonize disparate energies to create reason while balancing emotions and helping heal family tensions. Give tiger's eye its befitting high-ranking place on your altar.

Chakra correspondence: *Root, sacral,* and *solar plexus,* which, combined, give us serene, powerful confidence to manifest intentions and the courage and creativity to overcome anything blocking our path.

— TOPAZ —

Today, I choose joy and confidence. I am sovereign of my universe.

Topaz, an aluminum silicate mineral, is one of the most storied stones in gem lore. It is a magnet for love and affection and is said to hold the ability to cure more ills than any other stone. Naturally found in a rainbow of colors, the steadfast blue topaz is actually colorless topaz that's been treated to achieve the blue color. If you're born in November, you can proudly wear topaz as your birthstone.

Magical force: Topaz radiates joy and is a crystal of manifestation. This stone promotes honesty, inner wisdom, peace, and openness, making it particularly helpful in meditation work. It's also credited with curing insomnia; manifesting luck and exquisite beauty; attracting wealth; protecting from evil; bestowing long life, good health, strength, and stamina; improving vision or affording invisibility; preventing nightmares; increasing willpower; boosting energy; and even supporting weight loss—it will help rid your life of anything not serving its highest purpose! Whatever your magical inclinations or desires, topaz rocks the energy and can help you achieve them.

Chakra correspondence: *All*, due to topaz's rainbow of color options available.

TOURMALINE

I am a multihued being, capable of accomplishing anything I put my mind to.

Tourmaline, in all its sparkling clear beauty, comes in a rainbow of hues (the ancient Egyptians thought tourmaline passed through a rainbow at some point during its formation), including more than one color in a single stone! Its colors are created by the various minerals, such as copper, iron, manganese, or titanium, which are included in the crystals and affect their overall chemical makeup. Discovered by conquistadors in Brazil in the 1500s, it was originally mistaken for emerald. In any color, however, tourmaline is a powerful crystal. If you're an October baby, tourmaline is an alternative birthstone for opal.

Magical force: A loving, positive stone, tourmaline allows the release of tension and is credited with giving one self-confidence and wisdom as well as a boost to intuition. Tourmaline gives you the ability to eloquently communicate your thoughts and feelings. If gripped by fear of grief, tourmaline may help ease the emotional pain that accompanies it. In addition:

- **Black tourmaline** can provide a potent, invisible shield of protection around you as well as ease stress and anxiety.

- ❧ **Blue tourmaline** fosters spiritual growth.

- ❧ **Brown tourmaline** has grounding energies and is incredibly powerful in breaking bad habits or growing new/good ones. It is a good all-purpose crystal for aura cleansing.

- ❧ **Green tourmaline**, when buried in a garden or flowerpot, encourages lush, healthy plants to bloom. Its power can connect you to Nature and its healing magic, including releasing negative emotions such as jealousy.

- ❧ **Orange tourmaline** lights the fires of creativity within.

- ❧ **Pink tourmaline** can help you communicate with angelic fairies and has naturally soothing properties that promote ease, compassion, and love.

- ❧ **Purple tourmaline**, like black tourmaline, affords protective energy against negative influences.

- ❧ **Red tourmaline** promotes energy and vitality.

- ❧ **Watermelon tourmaline**, with its fascinating combination of the energies of both green and pink tourmaline, draws beneficial spirits to you while empowering you to rid your life of anything preventing the manifestation of your goals.

- ❧ **Yellow tourmaline** radiates optimism and power.

Chakra correspondence: In general, tourmaline—particularly a tourmaline wand—is excellent for balancing the chakras and cleansing your aura. With its rainbow-hued assortment of colors, there is a tourmaline match for each chakra, which can be effective in working through specific problems or imbalances in energy flow.

─ TURQUOISE ─

The sky has no limit and neither do my talents.

Formed only in the driest places on Earth blessed with copper-rich groundwaters, this striking blue-green stone is like holding a piece of the sky. It is one of the world's most ancient gems, and civilizations across centuries have held this crystal sacred for its powers of wisdom and regal symbolism. Turquoise is believed to bring good health, good luck, and good fortune. Its lovely blue color and association with both air and water make turquoise the perfect stone for instilling a go-with-the-flow mind-set.

Turquoise has served ancient warriors and rulers as amulets and talismans, and has also been offered to gods and nobility. Those born in December can count turquoise among their birthstone choices.

Magical force: Turquoise is said to be a good luck charm that can balance emotions and ground you spiritually. It promotes serenity, relieves stress, blocks negative energy, and keeps you from overreacting in tense situations. Turquoise can remind you of what is important when you listen to your soul and to see *and accept* all that makes you *you*.

Chakra correspondence: *Third eye*—heightens spiritual attunement and promotes clear spiritual communication; *throat*—channels wisdom and helps you speak your truth easily.

Meditations, Rituals & Spells

You've learned how crystal magic, like other types of magic aligned with Nature, helps you focus, amplify, and orchestrate energies, working with the Universe to influence and manifest outcomes in your magical life. It is another tool, just like the spells you cast to help bring your intentions to reality, to living a fulfilled and intention-filled life, aligned with Nature and her energies—to let the magic flow.

In this chapter are thirty-three suggestions for meditations, rituals, and spells for use in combination with your crystals to achieve the sparkling, beautiful, mesmerizing, bewitching, dreamy, successful, easy, joyful life you envision.

CHAKRA RAINBOW CRYSTAL MEDITATION

*J*ust the faintest glimpse of a rainbow can instill us with immeasurable joy. Knowing you carry a rainbow within you, the color correspondences of your chakras, you can use their energy and this imagery to conjure happiness any time you need a mood lift or energy adjustment.

Select a crystal in each color of the rainbow—red, orange, yellow, green, blue, indigo, and violet—the colors that bridge Earth to the heavens; the rainbow within you that bridges the power of your intentions and actions to your energy within. Hold the crystals, if you like, or align them in order in front of you from root chakra to crown chakra. While focusing on each crystal, one at a time, allow their energies to inspire joyful mantras to vibrate within and open your heart and mind to all that surrounds you. When ready, say quietly or aloud:

Breathe and believe: I am joy, I am light, I am peace.
Breathe and believe: I am strong, I am here, I am enough.
Breathe and believe: I have hope, I have love, I have all.

Find a peaceful, quiet location. Close your eyes, if you are comfortable doing so, and breathe in each color, one at a time, letting it fill you from head to toe as it instills you with its vitality and joy.

- Red: Breathe in passion; breathe out pain.

- Orange: Breathe in creativity; breathe out boredom.

- Yellow: Breathe in the joyful, life-giving qualities of the Sun; breathe out fear.

- Green: Breathe in renewal; breathe out sorrow.

- Blue: Breathe in calm; breathe out tension.

- Indigo: Breathe in intuition; breathe out negativity.

- Violet: Breathe in the messages of the Universe; breathe out gratitude.

CRYSTAL MAGIC IN 30 SECONDS

Thirty seconds may not seem like a lot of time (sit quietly, eyes closed, no agenda, set a timer and you'll see it's longer than you think!), but it's just enough to start, end, or rejuvenate your day with a burst of energy or a dose of calm to help you stay true to your goals and aligned with your intentions. Meditative crystal rituals do not have to be time-consuming or elaborate. They are intended to work for you and with you. Here are ten easy meditative spells you can use to keep the energy flowing even when time is of the essence. Gather your thoughts, some crystals, and thirty seconds. Magic is belief—and here we'll make it brief!

SLEEP

Peaceful, restful, rejuvenating sleep is a must for any busy person to stay focused, alert, productive—and magical. It's also a necessary form of self-care, especially if you take care of others. This is a great mini-ritual for the end of the day, or nap time.

Amethyst, angelite, celestite, lepidolite, rainbow moonstone, and selenite provide calming, balancing, and soothing vibrations and can help purify any negative energy around or within, so you can surrender your worries and let sleep drift in, or grab a crystal that feels calming to you. Place the crystal under your pillow, get comfortable, visualize the crystal's calming vibrations gently lulling you to dreamland, and drift off with these thoughts:

Relax, recharge, release. Sweet sleep bring restful peace.

EASE

Not all crystals amp up the vibrations. Select these calming crystals to channel stress away from your day and make room for ease and relaxation to take its place: choose amethyst, blue lace agate, celestite, clear quartz, fluorite, moonstone, rose quartz, or shungite.

If your stress or anxiety is something you're managing throughout the day, find a stone you can wear or carry with you, or place in your workspace, car, or wherever you've been spending time. When you feel the need for a respite, sit quietly holding your crystal and absorbing its calming resonance. Take a deep breath in through your nose, filling your lungs as fully as you can, hold it, visualize your breath absorbing the stress you're holding, and then slowly breathe out the negative energy. Take another deep breath in—one of ease, light, and calm—to fill the space left. Say quietly or aloud:

Of crystal's light and ease I'm filled,
releasing all that hurts and serves no good.

— PATIENCE —

The patience of a saint . . . not an easy trait to practice in our overbooked, hectic, uncertain world, but one that would ease the stress of the day invaluably. Taking time each day to remind ourselves of the value of patience, which breeds generosity, tolerance, and overall happiness, is an investment that pays huge returns. Amber, clear quartz, emerald, and sapphire are excellent crystal companions for fostering patience. With your crystal in hand, count slowly to ten, then say quietly or aloud:

These crystals, grown through time and stress,
prove life does shape us to our best.
A little patience shown today returns threefold in endless ways.

A DASH OF INTENTION

Living a life of intentional magic supported by crystal energy·is a beautiful thing. A simple way to season your days with the power of your intentions is to infuse your food while cooking, and then to eat mindfully, savoring the flavors, sensations, textures, aromas, and nourishment for both body and soul. Whether you season with salt while cooking or to finish the food before eating, take a brief pause to reflect on what you're working to manifest in life, give thanks for your abundance already in existence, and sprinkle intention into your meal to conjure a bit more magic. When ready, say quietly or aloud:

I season this food with salt that its best flavor may shine. I season this food with intention that achieved outcomes are mine. So mote it be.

GROUNDED FOR GOOD

When you feel at odds with everything and everyone around you, it's time to call time-out. Take a moment to ground your energies, releasing any negative thoughts, worries, or fears, and then continue on from a position of power. Smoky quartz is your best bet here.

Holding the crystal in your hands, with your feet firmly planted on the ground, visualize all the disruptive negativity being transferred to the stone. When ready, say quietly or aloud:

I release all unbalanced energy into this crystal and welcome stable energy in its place. I am grounded in confidence and power.

Place the stone outside, where it will diffuse the negativity into Earth and be transformed into energy for growth.

DRAW THE LINE

Many of us get caught in the cycle of spending our time tending to others' needs—boss, partner, children, friends, parents, coworkers, even pets—with little time left for ourselves.

Sometimes, our calendars are just too full and sometimes the fear of saying "no," and displeasing someone, prevents us from taking our own side. Healthy boundaries are critical to self-care, starting with self-protection and maintaining emotional stability. Amethyst, chrysocolla, garnet, rose quartz, smoky quartz, and tiger's eye can all be allies in establishing some "me time" for self-care. Meditating with your chosen crystals is an effective first step. When ready, say quietly or aloud:

Invisible shield, surround me with your might
that undisturbed I be until ready to reunite.

SUCCESS

When you want to ensure the win lands squarely in your column, taking a moment to make sure you have the correct, open-to-success mind-set is the crucial first step. Crystals that can help kick a self-defeating attitude to the curb and attune your vibrations to one of abundance include citrine, green jade, labradorite, and tiger's eye. Sitting with your chosen crystals, imagine the success you wish to manifest. When ready, say quietly or aloud:

There is no limit to what the Universe provides.
I am grateful for all I have and worthy of all I achieve.
Choices are abundant: I choose success.

INTUITION

We all have it. We just don't all heed it, and there's no excuse for not honing it. Your intuition can be your best guide and protector when there's too much information to take in all at once or too little time to synthesize it all. Trust that divine wisdom you've been blessed with. And although there are a number of stones that can enhance intuition, lapis lazuli is one of the best to make it heard. When doubt begins to erode your natural instincts, hold lapis and say quietly or aloud:

With crystal clarity I accept what the eyes
cannot see but the heart knows is true.

SUCCESSFUL SPELLWORK

Use what spells speak to you, modify to suit your
needs, or create your own glittering spells. You have
the magic within to accomplish anything your heart
desires, and it's time to let it shine!

FEELING CONFIDENT

That self-possessed feeling that one is in control, has what it takes, and all will work out right takes us far in the world. For those times when a little "fake it 'til you make it" is required, wear your sparkliest bling or keep a trusted touchstone with you. Good options, among many, for boosting the confidence factor and helping you put your surest foot forward include agate, amazonite, carnelian, citrine, hematite, and opal. When ready to call the confident self to the present, take a deep breath, exhale fully, then say quietly or aloud:

Grounded in belief am I that deep beneath the surface lies the strength to face what life does ask: I'm doubly equal to the task.

GOOD DAY!

To spark a little joy and get the day off on the right foot, a quick crystal magic spell with sunny citrine will make you smile and remind you of all you have to be grateful for—even on the gloomiest of days. Let your sparkle help make someone else's day a little brighter, too. When ready, say quietly or aloud:

I bask in citrine's sun-filled rays, absorbing joy in every way, for blessed I am in many ways, I greet the sun this brand-new day.

CRYSTAL SLEEPY TIME BATH RITUAL

Sleep is not a luxury—it is a necessity for the body, mind, and soul to reset, recharge, and renew, to live to our fullest potential each day. It can also be elusive. For those times when the mind won't quiet, or the dreams do scare, or the body rebels against relaxing, try this ritual bath to ease into sleep's sweet embrace.

Water's flowing energy is a powerful companion to crystals' healing properties and setting intentions in motion. Gather the crystals that help you de-stress, release, relax, and feel safe and protected. There are many, including amethyst, angelite, black tourmaline, celestite, moonstone, rose quartz, sapphire, and selenite. Place any water-safe crystals in the tub and arrange the others around you, on the tub's ledge, on the floor, on a nearby table or stand, or, if there is room, on a special sleepy time crystal grid or altar in the room.

1. Set your intention for restful sleep and peaceful dreams.

2. Draw a warm bath. While the tub fills and the crystals infuse the water with their soothing energies, light a candle—white for purity and cleansing or blue for peace and serenity. Let the flame be the beacon that proclaims your intentions to the Universe.

3. Diffuse a relaxing essential oil or add a few drops to the bath, if you like, then slip into the water's healing embrace. Relax and close your eyes. Feel the water's gentle warmth and softness cradling you.

4. Breathe. Deeply in. Slowly out. Again.

5. Focus your thoughts on filling your body with the crystals' calming ease on every breath in. With every breath out, feel the stress, worry, fear, or strain flow into the water and be absorbed by the crystals around you. Feel yourself relax, grow heavy, and accepting of sleep's call. When ready to call sleep to your side, say quietly or aloud:

Soft water soothe and cleanse my soul, my body, heart, and mind,
With crystal charms to tame my dreams, it's rest I most desire.
I call sweet sleep to lie with me, to sing a lullaby—
To wake renewed, with energy to set the world on fire.

6. Stay as long as is comfortable and gently retune to the world around you when finished.

7. Drain the tub, feeling release as you visualize the stress and worries absorbed by the water and pulled from the stones disappear down the drain.

8. Gently dry the crystals in gratitude for their help and place them near your bed to softly lull you into restful sleep. Goodnight.

A Ritual for Any Intention

A bathing ritual can be a welcome respite of self-care any day. When you don't feel you have time in your busy schedule to fit one in, consider the double duty it can perform. Simply change the intention and match the crystals to it and you create a space in your life for self-care and reflection, with the intent of furthering your goals and manifesting intentions. Powerful magic, indeed.

SALTY RITUAL FOR CLEANSING AND PROTECTION

We've learned that salt can be an effective cleanser for your crystals (see page 31) and, as a crystal itself, it is powerfully energetic and a staple tool of any magic-practicing being. It is readily available and ready to serve in whatever way you desire. Here, we'll use salt in a simple ritual to keep spaces spiritually cleansed and vibrating for their highest good.

1. Fill a small glass bowl with salt (any kind will work, but plain table salt is most economical). Select an essential oil with strong cleansing energies, such as basil, bergamot, lavender, lemon, orange, peppermint, sage, or ylang-ylang, and add drops to the salt until you have the desired level of scent. The aroma will not only remind you when it's time to change the salt (when the scent is gone) but also adds to the cleansing process.

2. Place the bowl (safely out of reach of animals or children in the home) in the room you need cleansed, such as where someone has been ill, or company has stayed, or an argument

has taken place, or that you avoid because you just don't like how it feels, and say quietly or aloud:

I place this salt for all to see that evil, ills, and sadness be absorbed into its very core so harm is pulled far from my door.

3. Repeat the ritual anywhere and everywhere as needed, as often as needed. Dispose of the salt mindfully by washing it down the drain and visualizing the water absorbing the salt and negativity as it flows down and away from you.

‧⁀C‧ **PROTECTION SPELL** ‧Ɔ⁀‧

For that invisible cloak of unbreakable protection surrounding you and your home, black tourmaline is your ally. Whether an energetic sabotage from a jealous coworker or pressure-packed meetings, vexing (or hexing) neighbors, self-doubt, or general unease, black tourmaline can block, purify, and reflect negative energies, allowing you to breathe easier and go about your business confident of the outcomes. Tuck a stone in your pocket, place one by your front door, or position one on your desk, and give thanks for this protective friend. A few words to direct your intentions can amplify its properties.

*Under your spell I remain undeterred, for cloaked in
your charms I am safe and assured.*

HESTIA • FIRE AGATE = BLESSED HOME

Call upon the Greek goddess of hearth and home, Hestia (Vesta to the Romans), the original domestic goddess, to bless your home for happy lives. Fire agate is the perfect crystal to add to this blessing. Its ancient lore tells us that the origins of fire itself burn within. To keep the home fires burning bright and your family nurtured and nourished, gaze into fire agate's burning beauty, raise a glass in her honor (it's tradition!), and say to Hestia, quietly or aloud:

This fire agate radiates the warmth of Hestia's grace.
I pray to her that warmed we'll be within this sacred space.
Extend your blessings on this home, that love burns always bright;
Keep watch, dear goddess, keep us safe within your guiding light.

MOONSTONE MAGIC FOR MANIFESTING DREAMS

When the power of moonstone and the powerful Full Moon combine, your magical spellwork can soar. On the night of the next Full Moon, gather your moonstone and stand, illuminated, in the Moon's abundant light. Let it shine into your heart to reveal your most desired intentions. When ready, say quietly or aloud:

I call upon the Moon's insight, with moonstone by my side,
to open wide my heart and eyes that I may recognize
the gifts of great abundance or other cherished prize
when manifest within my life, those dreams that never died.

SUNNY OPTIMISM

Sunny-colored citrine is one of the best crystal companions for instilling an optimistic outlook and filling your heart with joy. If you've been feeling a bit glass-half-empty these days, pick up citrine to change your outlook. Remember, like attracts like, and a positive outlook will draw positive things to you. What are you waiting for? Holding your crystal, when ready, say quietly or aloud, as many times as you need:

I am filled with warmth. I am filled with joy.
Each sunrise beams gratitude into my heart.

TRUE LOVE

I f things feel a little lackluster in the romance department and it's what's missing from a fully magical life, open your heart and mind to the many possibilities around you. Turn to your crystals for a little energy nudge to get things flowing. Consider arranging them by your bedside, sleeping with them under your pillow, or creating an altar set up in your bedroom dedicated to love and romance. Clear your crystals before working with them, set your intentions, and offer thanks for their help. Choose:

- **Amethyst** soothes conflict, if that's what's in love's way.

- **Blue lace agate**, which speaks from the heart, helps with honest communication and building trust to establish a new relationship, or rebuild one anew.

- **Chrysocolla** can help you be rid of bad habits—including bad relationships—if that's your obstacle to finding true love. It can also be used in love spells, to open your heart to the joy of new beginnings.

- **Diamond** declares your intention of everlasting love to the Universe . . . be open to its response.

- **Garnet** stimulates passion, communicates your desires to your intended, and inspires sweep-me-off-my-feet romance.

- **Malachite** helps heal past hurts and opens your heart—and heart chakra—and mind to accept love again.

- **Rose quartz** reminds you to love yourself first; others will love you in return.

- **Sunstone** burns with a passion for life, igniting what makes you truly happy . . . love will follow.

Crystals burning bright with love, conjure passion with your charms.
Cast your spell that lovers do unite their hearts, make time to woo.
Create a glow to draw them near, their eyes to meet, their souls to sear.
Of one true love you do portend, spark a flame that knows no end.

SOULMATE MATCH

If your wish is to attract the perfect match, green jade, a crystal of ease and harmony, can get you vibrating in sync with your soul mate. Ensure you're both on the same wavelength when it comes to conjuring love and romance with this simple spell. While in your search, keep this, your chosen stone, with you at all times. When ready, say quietly or aloud:

With jade's luster may I shine to signal that I'm here,
and vibrate with a tempting song that draws my lover near.
Those dear sweet words of whispered love breathed softly in my ear
that say I'm irresistible are what I want to hear.

FORGIVENESS

Forgiveness is a powerful balm but can sometimes be elusive. Whether it's yourself you're striving to forgive or someone close to you, or you're seeking that all-healing forgiveness from another, rhodochrosite can help. Its tender energies will boost your self-love and acceptance, empowering you to forgive yourself and learn from your mistakes, then giving you the compassion to open yourself to loving others, especially those who may also need your forgiveness. When ready to begin healing, while holding rhodochrosite, or another stone of forgiveness, say quietly or aloud:

With humble heart, I vow to see the truth of my mistakes.
With human heart, I show myself forgiving, healing grace.
With loving heart, forgiveness means that love will take pain's place.

TRUTH AND TRUST

Without truth there is no trust, and without trust there are no relationships. Truth and trust go hand in hand and whether the truth is yours to tell or hear, it can sometimes be difficult to face. But speaking or hearing the truth, always delivered with care, actually resolves more conflict than it creates. So, when you need an ally to hold you accountable for truth and the courage to trust your truth as well as any told to you, turn to your favorite blue crystals, such as blue lace agate, celestite, lapis lazuli, or sapphire. Holding your chosen crystal, take a moment to center and ground yourself. When ready, say quietly or aloud:

I speak with truth. I hear with truth.
I act with truth. I love with truth.
I trust the truth of the Universe and its plan for me.

✦ LET IT GO! ✦

W hen you just can't shake those worries loose, it's time
for a bit of crystal clarity—so, pack up those troubles
and let them go! Amethyst, with its soothing energies, can help.
Holding the stone, take a few deep, calming breaths. Focus on the
worries you'd like to release and feel the stone absorbing them.
When ready, say quietly or aloud:

Worries, woes, and burdens, I release you into this stone.
I fill my cleared mind with amethyst's soothing powers.
I let go of all that does not serve.

Repeat as often as needed to keep anxiety at bay. Cleanse the
stone before its next use, placing it near a window where the
Moon's cleansing energies will clear the stone, or in a glass of
clean water to pull out the negative energy and recharge it.

⋯ LOSE THE BLUES ⋯

Sometimes pulling yourself out of a blue mood is easier said than done. Working every day to be the best version of yourself is not easy work and can sometimes feel overwhelming. Add life's natural ups and downs to the mix and it's easy to retreat into a blue funk of avoidance. While it may feel good temporarily, you can't stay there. Invite sunny sunstone for a healing chat and try a little crystal talk therapy. Sunstone radiates positivity and protection without judgment and can help pull you from the darkness into the light. While holding sunstone to your heart, envision a moment that you felt joyful, reveling in the emotion. Holding that joy, when ready, say quietly or aloud:

I seek the warmth of sunshine on my face to dry the tears.
I need the peace of living life that doesn't dwell in fear.
I ask to be uplifted and to feel my burdens ease,
I'm ready to reclaim my joy and leave behind dis-ease.

WASH IT AWAY!

When life's frazzle-dazzle has you spinning like a top, use this simple ritual to ease your troubles down the drain. Gather your most calming, water-safe crystal and a soft towel. Working near a sink, holding your crystal, take a moment to focus your intentions on what you'd like to rid from your world and imagine the sense of ease you'll have when it's gone. Gently rinse the crystal and your hands under running water, holding gratitude for the clean water and cleansing crystal energies, while silently visualizing any troubles being washed away. Dry the crystal and your hands and take a moment to breathe in the ease. When ready, say quietly or aloud:

Nerves be soothed with water's ease; bother be gone, refreshed I'll be.
Crystal cleansed of ills and woe, restore my world with magic glow.

⚮ IT'S TIME! ⚮

Whatever you thought of when you read that title is exactly what you need to tackle with this spell. Procrastination will get you nowhere fast, and it's a sign your solar plexus chakra is out of balance and your self-esteem is, too. So, whatever it is you've been ruminating on, and for whatever reason, pyrite, or another yellow- or gold-colored crystal, can help you get unstuck, turning those thoughts into actions. When ready, say quietly or aloud:

Tick-tock, the clock has run its course—there's no time left to waste.
Prepared am I to spark the flame that lights the need for haste.
The ancient flame burns bright within to let my warrior shine.
It's time to take control of life: achievement will be mine.

TIGER STRENGTH

Tigers are among the most powerful cats on Earth and they possess a keen sense of vision—equally as good day or night. When your circumstances call for a fierce demeanor and ability to see clearly to keep your eyes on the prize, invite tiger's eye to your side to take down the competition. Wear or carry tiger's eye with you when the stakes are high and you want to come out on top. Take a deep breath, and say quietly or aloud:

With tiger's eye held to my heart, it beats with courage anew
to leap with faith at what I want and strength to see it through.
With ease and grace despite the pace, I claim what I pursue.

⤜ᘓ · SUCCESS! · ᘒ⤛

We all want it. We all dream of it. Success. But what it means to each of us is different and dependent on so many circumstances. However you define it, success is something we all deserve and can achieve with an open mind and a focus on manifesting intentions. Numerous crystals can facilitate the drive for success; here, we'll call on pyrite because it manifests tangible results that are proof of our success. So, while gazing into your crystal, form a picture in your mind of the success you desire. When ready, say quietly or aloud:

I open my mind to new meanings of success.
I open my heart to accept success.
I open my hands to receive success.
I open my eyes to see opportunities for success.
I open my ears to the sweet sound of success.
I open my life to live with success.

Place the crystal where you will see it, and embrace its constant reminder of the success you have achieved. Honor the work you do to bring more success into your life. Repeat as needed.

GOOD LUCK

Even though solid preparation is the best predictor of luck, chance certainly plays a role . . . and why just leave luck to chance?! To increase your odds of a lucky break, as luck would have it, aventurine is your lucky charm. Wear or carry your crystal and get ready to make your own luck. When ready, say quietly or aloud:

With crystal in hand I feel lucky indeed, said three times the charm:
Of luck I'm in need.
Whether luck of the Irish, the draw, or beginner,
I call on this stone to ensure I'm a winner!

COMMIT TO CHANGE

Making changes, especially to establish new, healthier habits, is hard. And despite claims that a new habit can be established in twenty-one days, there is really no hard-and-fast rule. What is known, though, is that it takes repetition and commitment. And, since crystal magic is already a habit, why not combine it with the desire to change and increase the odds of it sticking? Crystal partners to help you banish the bad habit and usher in the new include amazonite, amethyst, black onyx, chrysocolla, clear quartz, fairy stones, kyanite, and tiger's eye.

But, remember, always use what speaks to you. Set your intention to change clearly and strongly, then get ready to program it into your chosen crystal for help. When ready, say quietly or aloud:

With crystals to aid this hope in my heart, I seek here
to banish what's bad from the start.
I pray that new habits, repeated, take hold and bring
forth the change that turns new into old.
To gather the strength to do this each day,
I call on this crystal to show me the way.

GET CREATIVE

When your creative well is dry, it's time to look beyond the usual places for inspiration. Some of Nature's gifts to refill our creative reserves include Herkimer diamond and celestite—used together for optimum results. The ancient, double-terminated Herkimer diamond is able to transmit as well as receive information beyond any that we know, and the high-vibrational activity of both stones helps attune you to a higher realm. You'll be open to new ideas and feel the spirits guide you with their divine inspiration. When ready, place your hands over the crystals and say quietly or aloud:

I feel the energies from times past stir memories in my core, which grow and reach and fill that niche that's empty in my soul.
A light takes hold, revealing secrets hidden in my heart, that yearn to see the light of day and signal a new start.
The spirits whisper words so sweet, erasing any fear:
Don't hesitate—the world awaits . . . from you they long to hear.

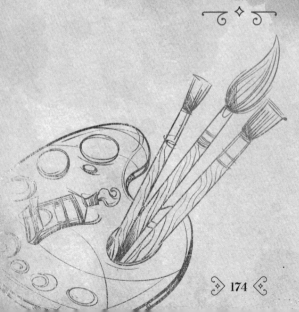

REVEAL THE FUTURE

When a glimpse into the future might help you deal with the realities of today, gather your crystal seers to raise your sense of clairvoyance. Angelite, azurite, blue kyanite, green tourmaline, labradorite, malachite, moonstone, selenite, and sodalite are but a few of the stones that can boost your intuition and heighten your clairvoyance. Building your intuitive skills can help you navigate questions when working on long-term goals and give you a quick gut check on those everyday issues that pop up.

- Place your crystals in the spaces you inhabit most frequently and let their energies retune yours.

- Wear or carry them, or just sit with your crystals each day, focusing on your intentions and questions, for a more personal experience.

- Use them to clear your chakras, to unlock your internal channels of communication.

- Sleep with them, asking for guidance in your dreams.

- Create a crystal grid (see page 72) devoted to clairvoyance.

- Meditate with your crystals to work through specific issues.

While building your clairvoyance capacity, be open to receiving the energies and messages that abound around you. When ready to begin, say quietly or aloud:

I seek to know beyond the known, to see what I don't see.
To have the gift of knowing sight bestowed this day on me.

Ready to put your skills to work? When seeking a peek into the future, cast a circle with your crystals, form the question in your mind, and say quietly or aloud:

To guide my actions and my fate and hint of what's to come I wait.

⟨ᴄ · **EMBRACE YOUR INNER GODDESS** · ɔ⟩

rystals and goddesses are an enchanting combination. Every day brings with it opportunities to tap into your divine feminine goddess powers for doing good in the world and living your true, authentic life. Enhanced by crystal energy, let your goddess aura shine brightly into the world, where it will create its own magic. And whether you just want to be worshiped for the goddess you are or be the ruler of your own crystal magic world, there's a goddess and symbolic crystal for that. Here's a list to help you get started.

LOVE & BEAUTY

Eos (Greek) Titan Goddess of the Dawn / Aurora (Roman) / Tesana (Etruscan)	Agate
Freya (Norse)	Red jasper
Hebe (Greek) / Juventas (Roman)	Bloodstone
Inanna (Sumerian/Mesopotamian)	Amber
Venus (Roman) / Aphrodite (Greek)	Rose quartz, sodalite

MARRIAGE, FERTILITY & MOTHERHOOD

Corn Mother (Native American) / Demeter (Greek) / Ceres (Roman)	Moss agate
Cybele (Phrygian)	Red quartz
Danu (Celtic)	Lapis lazuli, opal, sodalite
Hera (Greek) / Juno (Roman)	Garnet, lapis lazuli
Isis (Egyptian)	Carnelian
Mawu (West African)	Moonstone
Ninhursag (Sumerian)	Amber, malachite
Oshun (African)	Coral
Selene (Greek) / Luna (Roman)	Moonstone
Yemaya (African)	Mother-of-pearl, turquoise

RELATIONSHIPS, TRUTH & FORGIVENESS

Amaterasu (Japanese)	Pyrite
Clementia (Roman) / Eleos (Greek)	Rose quartz
Iris (Greek)	Rainbow quartz
Kuan Yin (Chinese)	Jade
Ma'at (Egyptian)	Clear quartz
Rhiannon (Welsh)	Sapphire
Veritas (Roman) / Aletheia (Greek)	Blue apatite

HOME, HEART & HEALING

Airmid (Celtic)	Amber, fairy stone
Bao Gu (Chinese)	Clear quartz
Brigid (Celtic)	Angelite
Cerridwen (Celtic)	Sunstone
Epione (Greek)	Aquamarine
Frigg (Norse)	Emerald, moonstone
Gabija (Lithuanian)	Salt
Hestia (Greek) / Vesta (Roman)	Fire agate
Nidra (Hindu)	Amethyst

ABUNDANCE, GOOD FORTUNE & PROSPERITY

Berchta (Germanic)	Diamond
Fortuna (Roman) / Tyche (Greek)	Citrine
Lakshmi (Hindu)	Diamond
Pachamama (Andean)	Petrified wood
Rosmerta (Celtic)	Crystal-carved dish

WISDOM & KNOWLEDGE

Anahita (Persian)	Emerald
Hecate (Greek)	Black tourmaline
Seshat (Egyptian)	Carnelian
Snotra (Norse)	Small pile of rocks or stones: any
Sophia (Greek) / Hokmah (Hebrew)	Blue kyanite, sodalite

STRENGTH & PROTECTION

Bastet/Bast (Egyptian)	Tiger's eye
Diana (Roman) / Artemis (Greek)	Amethyst, moonstone
Durga (Hindu)	Carnelian
Nike (Greek) / Victoria (Roman)	Hematite
Tara (Hindu) / Sgrol-ma (Buddhist)	Aventurine

CREATIVITY & JOY

Athena (Greek) / Minerva (Roman)	Lapis lazuli
Hathor (Egyptian)	Malachite
Baubo / Iambe (Greek)	Obsidian
Ixchel (Mayan)	Pink sapphire
Saraswati, also Sarasvati (Hindu) / Benzaiten (Japanese)	Watermelon tourmaline

When you've decided on the goddess path you'd like to walk, take your crystal in hand, invite your chosen goddess to walk with you, and say quietly or aloud:

O goddess wise, hear my plea, enhanced by crystals meant for thee:
When goddess power reveals the hour to let my magic shine,
it's now or never to share my treasure and spread my gifts around.
I seek to rule my realm with love and boundless goddess charm,
To summon strength when times are hard and keep all safe
from any harm.

· TRAVEL TALISMANS ·

Whether for business or pleasure, travel can be enormously rewarding and a chance to broaden our views of the world. It can also be stressful and, literally, make us sick. There is so much beyond our control when traveling that even the most prepared among us can feel lost at sea. Just as you carefully pack your clothes and toiletries, make sure not to leave crystals out of the equation. Deciding which comforting friends to leave home just may be the hardest part. Consider:

- **Amber**, for patience and grounding
- **Amethyst**, to combat stressful emotions, restore joy, and encourage restful sleep
- **Black tourmaline**, for protection from bad vibes and other negative energies wherever they come from, and to strengthen the immune system
- **Blue kyanite**, to keep your intuition working at full peak
- **Garnet**, for safe travel (even Noah had one on the Ark!)
- **Green jade**, for good luck
- **Hematite**, to take in and learn from new experiences you have
- **Labradorite**, to embrace change
- **Lapis lazuli**, to keep calm and carry on
- **Malachite**, for help with fear of flying
- **Moonstone**, for adapting to the ebb and flow of changing schedules and routines and to keep you uplifted
- **Peacock ore**, to attract all good things to you
- **Rose quartz**, for compassion—and good sleep!

- **Selenite**, for its cleansing properties

- **Spirit quartz**, to open your mind and heart to new experiences

- **Sunstone**, for an optimistic outlook

- **Tiger's eye**, to manage fear

- **Topaz**, to manifest the outcomes you desire

While packing your chosen crystals for travel, take a moment to imbue them with their intended work, then when ready, say quietly or aloud:

I ask these crystals to journey with me,
that far and wide wherever I be,
the skies are clear, the seas are calm; the mood's of joy;
I'm safe from harm.
To learn from all I meet and see, to grow from our diversity.
Return me home, the same but new,
for widened now is my worldview.

Upon this journey's end we've come,
I hope you've learned and grown—
found something in these crystal friends
of magic so foretold.

For in their hearts these crystals beat
with stories of the past,
their energies ignite the meanings
of the spells we cast.

Take care to keep your stones tucked safe,
away from any harm. Their sparkle must remain
intact to work their magic charm.

Continue on, you're well prepared to dig yet deeper still,
to manifest the life you dream, each wish to be fulfilled.

The wisdom you've unlocked within is certain now to shine,
for versed in all their magic, crystals' secrets are now thine.

ACKNOWLEDGMENTS

Beginning each new book is a bit like gazing into a crystal ball—the image is fuzzy, but becomes clearer over time. My immense thanks to Quarto publisher, Rage Kindelsperger, for scrying a role for me in contributing to this magical series. It has been my pleasure.

I'm grateful for the energetic guidance of my editor, Elizabeth You, and to the rest of the Quarto teams: my sincere thanks for all you do to create and sell such beautiful books.

To my husband, John, my dearest treasure, thank you for your unfailing ability to see magic everywhere, and for sharing that vision with me. Your love and trust are truly inspiring, and you bring me joy unending each day.

To all my friends and family who cast magic into my life daily, thank you for your love and support.

Finally, the world would be such a dull place without the magic of books. It is a magic multiplied exponentially each time a reader opens one and brings their own magic to it. Thank you for spreading the magic.

RESOURCES AND REFERENCES

American Gem Society: AmericanGemSociety.org

Atkin, Emily. "Do You Know Where Your Healing Crystals Come From?" *New Republic*, May 11, 2018. https://newrepublic.com/article/148190/know-healing-crystals-come-from.

Cape Town Diamond Museum: CapeTownDiamondMuseum.org

Crystal Vaults: CrystalVaults.com

Energy Muse: EnergyMuse.com

Gemological Institute of America: GIA.edu

Geology.com

Hall, Judy. *101 Power Crystals*. Beverly, MA: Fair Winds Press, 2011.

Hall, Judy. *The Crystal Bible*. Iola, WI: Krause Publications, 2003.

Hall, Judy. *Crystals and Healing Stones*. New York: Barnes and Noble, 2006.

How Stuff Works: HowStuffWorks.com

International Gem Society: GemSociety.org

Kunz, George. *The Curious Lore of Precious Stones*. Philadelphia: J. B. Lippincott Company, 2013.

Legends of America: LegendsofAmerica.com

Martínez-Ripoll, Martin. "Crystallography-Cristalografia." https://www.xtal.iqfr.csic.es/Cristalografia/parte_01_1-en.html.

NASA: nasa.gov

National Geographic: NationalGeographic.com

O'Donnell, Lynne. "Afghanistan's Lapis Lazuli Seen as 'Conflict Mineral.'" AP News, June 6, 2016. https://apnews.com/article/7329dfca3680495db4bc674e184a1d26.

Reuters: Reuters.com

Sage Goddess: SageGoddess.com

Scientific American: ScientificAmerican.com

Smithsonian Magazine: SmithsonianMag.com

WitchcraftandWitches.com